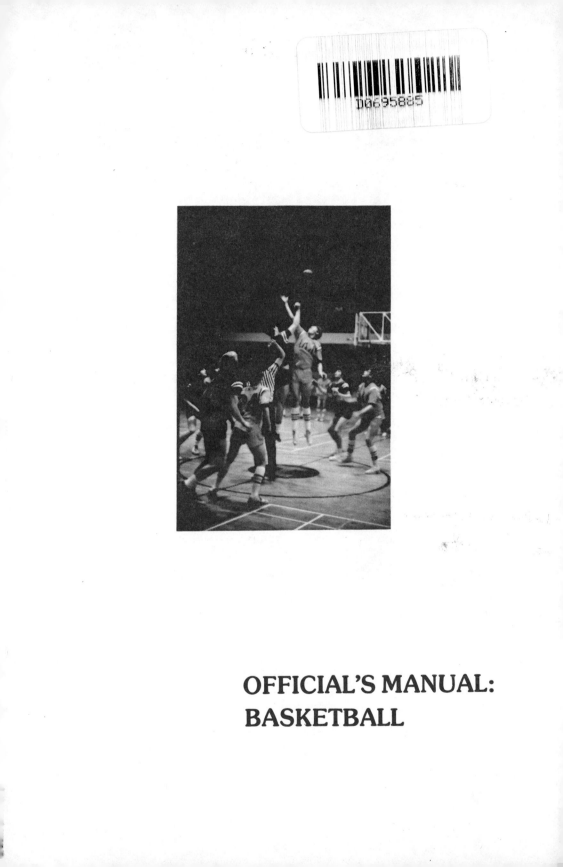

OFFICIAL'S MANUAL:
BASKETBALL

OFFICIAL'S MANUALS

from Leisure Press

TOUCH AND FLAG FOOTBALL

John W. Reznik
And Rod Grambeau
University of Michigan

1979/88 pp./paper $2.25
ISBN 0-918438-46-2

> **OFFICIAL'S MANUALS**
>
> only **$1.35** each on **1-time**
> purchase of **10 or more**
> copies (any combination)

BASKETBALL

Gary Miller
Cal State - Northridge

1979/72 pp./paper $2.25
ISNB 0-918438-47-0

VOLLEYBALL

James A. Peterson
And Lawrence S. Preo

1979/96 pp./paper $2.25
ISBN 0-918438-48-9

SOFTBALL

Robert Clickener
University of Illinois

1979/72 pp./paper $2.25
ISBN 0-918438-49-7

SOCCER

Nick Kovalakides
University of Maryland

1979/100 pp./paper $2.25
ISBN 0-918438-50-0

> • Use as a reference • Issue to your sports officials • A valuable aid for programs at *all* levels

OFFICIAL'S MANUAL:
BASKETBALL

includes:
- **OFFICIAL RULES**
- **MECHANICS**
- **ILLUSTRATED RULES**

Gary L. Miller

Leisure Press
P.O. Box 3
West Point, N.Y. 10996

A publication of Leisure Press.
P.O. Box 3, West Point, N.Y. 10996
Copyright © 1979 by Leisure Press
All rights reserved. Printed in the U.S.A.

ISBN 0-918438-47-0

Illustrations by Gini Pierson and David Rowe

Back cover design by Lanny Sommese

CONTENTS

The speed and complex design of basketball require instant and accurate decisions from the officials. (from the Preface.)

Preface

The quality of any sporting event is directly dependent upon the quality of the officiating that takes place in that event.

Basketball is one of the most difficult sports to officiate. Its speed and complex design require instant and accurate decisions from the officials. The fact that officials cannot take time to analyze what has happened demands a thorough knowledge of the rules, instant recognition of the situation and instinctive reactions. Add to the complexity and rapidity of the game, the high emotional level and proximity of spectators, and it is easily seen why basketball officiating requires a dedicated commitment from everyone involved in a particular game.

This material was gathered by the author in an attempt to provide the readers with guidelines to achieving consistency and uniformity in basketball officiating. The book places an emphasis on good officiating mechanics, because mechanics will provide every official with the basis for handling the vast number of possible situations that may arise in the game of basketball. In certain instances specific game situations will be presented with the idea that if an official has once been exposed to a situation and is informed of the proper response (call), the likelihood of that official handling that same situation correctly the second and all subsequent times is increased. Repetitive correct responses strengthen that response.

It is hoped that the information presented in this book will prove useful to instructors of sport officiating, officials, and spectators alike.

G.L.M.

CHAPTER I

Preliminaries To Basketball Officiating

Basketball courts vary in size from gymnasium to gymnasium; however, ideal measurements are 50' by 84' for high school age players and 50' by 94' for college age players. Sidelines and endlines mark the exterior boundaries of the court. It is important to note that not all basketball courts are marked with 2" lines. Some use a contrasting color to distinguish the out-of-bounds area from the in-bounds area. In the case of the court with 2" lines, the out-of-bounds area begins at a plane extending from the inside edge of the line vertically to the ceiling of the gymnasium. The contrasting color court's out-of-bounds area begins at the inside edge of the contrasting color and extends vertically from that point. Not shown on the diagram is the restraining line. This line is used only when there is less than 3' of unobstructed space outside the exterior boundaries of the court. The restraining line is a narrow (usually 1") broken line extending around the entire court 3' inside the boundary lines. This line functions as the boundary line during throw-ins.

The center circle is a circle located equal distance between the endlines and sidelines, having an inside radius of 2'. A restraining circle with an outside radius of 6' is drawn around the center circle.

A division line divides the court into two equal parts and passes through both sidelines and the center of the center circle. In the event the court is less than 74' in length, two separate division lines must be drawn. Each line is drawn 40' from the opposite endline.

A free-throw lane, 12' wide and 15' deep, shall be drawn at both ends of the court. These measurements shall be made from the outside of the 2" lines. Again, if a contrasting color is used, the boundaries of the free-throw lane begin at the outside edge of the contrasting color or line and extend in a vertical plane from that point. Lane-space marks and neutral-zone marks are placed along each side of the free-throw lane according to the dimensions shown on the diagram. Finally, two semi-circles are drawn using the free-throw line as a diameter. The semi-circle outside the lane is a solid 2" line, while the semi-circle inside the free-throw lane consists of 2" by 16" sections spaced 14" apart.

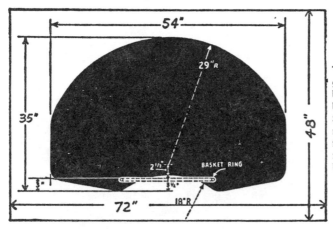

The diagram at left gives specifications for both types of back-boards. See Rule 1, Sections 7, 8, 9. It is not legal to paint a fan-shaped board on a rectangular back-board.

There are two types of backboards used in basketball; rectangular and fan-shaped. For both types of backboards, the front surface of the board must be flat. It shall be white in color unless the board is transparent. The rectangular board is 6' by 4', with the 4' being the vertical measurement. Fan-shaped backboards are 54" by 35" with specific variations shown on the diagram. If the board is transparent, a border of 3" in width for the rectangular board and 3", or less, in width for the fan-shaped board is required. A rectangle of 2" lines with outside measurements of 24" horizontally and 18" vertically shall be drawn with the top of the baseline level with the top edge of the ring. On the fan-shaped backboard, the baseline is omitted and the vertical lines extend to the bottom of the backboard. College teams should use a transparent, rectangular backboard, while all other teams may use either the rectangular or fan-shaped backboard in either transparent or non-transparent material.

Each backboard is located equal distance from the sidelines, with the front face perpendicular to the floor and parallel to the inside edge of the baseline. The backboard is placed 4' inside the baseline. The top of the rectangular backboard is 13' from the floor, and the top of the fan-shaped backboard is 12' 8" from the floor. The bottom edge and 15 inches up both sides of the rectangular backboard shall be padded with gray rubber or plastic shock-absorbing material not less than 2" thick.

Each basket shall consist of a single metal ring with an inside diameter of 18"; its flange and braces; and a white-cord, 12-mesh net, 15" to 18" in length, suspended from beneath the ring. The basket's upper edge shall be 10' above and parallel to the floor and shall be centered according to the vertical edges of the backboard.

Prerequisites

Good basketball officiating is the aim of coaches, players, fans, and officials alike. However, in order to reach the level of officiating desired, there are some prerequisites.

1. Knowledge of rules. Knowledge of the rules is absolutely essential to the good official. Maintaining this knowledge is equally important. Some officials assume that once certification from a local officials' association is obtained, their exposure to the rules has ended. Good officials not only review the rules before each season but also refer to special situations before and after each game. Rule changes in the game of basketball occur each year, and it is the responsibility of the official to keep abreast of these changes. The game of basketball is complicated and is constantly evolving from the first set of rules established in 1891. New interpretations and points of emphasis are presented with each year's new rule book. Keeping current with the rules requires the use of all available sources of information. Rule books, case books, illustrated rules, and handbooks are all excellent sources of current, accurate information. Commercial publications are another source of updated rule interpretations. Often these commercial publications contain pre-season questions and answers in the form of quizzes. Such quizzes are helpful in evaluating your knowledge of the rules and their year-to-year changes. Films and slides provide another excellent source of updating your knowledge. These are often presented by local or state associations with discussion periods to clarify any points of interest not presented, or not presented clearly, in the visual presentation. Use of these sources and a sincere effort by the official will insure a thorough and current knowledge of the rules of the game.

Knowledge of the rules as written in the rule book is obviously desirable; however, proper application of this knowledge to the game situation is essential to good officiating. The rules were written to insure that neither team is given an unfair advantage. They were written to insure fair play. The intent of the rules should be foremost in the philosophy of all good officials. Technical rule infractions occur during every minute of the average basketball game. If each and every one of these infractions were called by the official, the game would soon become a farce. It is the experienced and wise official who is instantly able to convert the *intent* of the rule to fit the situation. The overriding consideration should be whether one player gained an unfair advantage over his opponent. This guiding principle allows the game to be played with the fair and fast-paced action its inventor intended.

2. Physical Fitness. It has been calculated that a basketball official runs approximately five miles in an average game, and much of this running is done backwards. Therefore, the official desiring peek performance must actively engage himself in a pre-season training procedure similar to that of the athlete. Jogging and calisthenic exercises are both excellent methods of increasing cardio-vascular efficiency and improving endurance. These activities also improve muscle tone and, therefore, appearance.

A more specific way to improve physical fitness, while also fulfilling some of the other prerequisites for officiating, is the scrimmage. Each coach plans pre-season practice to include several scrimmage games. These may be intra-squad or between schools. A scrimmage provides a practice ground for the offical to sharpen rusty skills and is also an excellent fitness program. It is a good idea to take other officials to pre-season scrimmages so that the process of attaining the desired physical fitness can be a gradual one.

Fatigue is the enemy of all good officials. Not only does it rob him of his ability to insure proper coverage of the court physically, but it also impairs the ability to exercise good judgment. It slows the reaction time between the perception of a given situation and the appropriate response to that situation. Fatigue and its effects can best be minimized by maintaining the high level of physical fitness required to properly officiate the game of basketball.

3. Good Judgment. Because a great deal of "calls" made by a basketball official are "judgment calls," good judgment is a very important ingredient in the make-up of a good official. Some authors have stated that judgment cannot be taught. They feel it is an inherited quality; the official either has it or he doesn't. This is not completely true. Good judgment is the ability to see a situation and to make the correct response to that situation. Good judgment is made up of three parts: perception, position and experience. Perception is the ability to look at a situation and ascertain what is truly taking place. It is the ability to block out competing visual and audio stimuli and to devote complete attention to the situation at hand. True perception is not possible from an improper position. The official with the best judgment in the world cannot exercise his judgment unless he is in the correct position to insure true perception. When perception is learned and proper position insured, experience becomes the best teacher of good judgment. The ability to concentrate on specific areas where rule violations occur is a continuing process for the good official. The ability to look past the extraneous action and to pinpoint rapid movement of the foot or the slap of a hand is enhanced every time that particular situation is presented to the official. Identical to the learning of any skill, the presentation of a situation and the eliciting of the correct response increase the likelihood of that same response being elicited the next time that situation is encountered.

4. Consistency. Coaches and players often mention inconsistency as the most upsetting quality an official can possess. Consistent interpretation and administration of the rules are probably the most important qualities an official can demonstrate. True consistency does not mean attempting to equalize the rule interpretations for both teams, but rather interpreting each situation as a distinct, separate part of the game. The previous call, or the next call to be made, should not have any influence upon the situation under consideration. Consistency means to call a repeated play in the fourth period the same way you call it after the tip-off to start the game.

No two officials possess the same judgment; therefore, there will be individual differences from official to official. The good basketball official should strive to be internally consistent. This internal consistency allows you to view the same situation the same way each time it appears. Teams may not agree or be accustomed to a particular official's style, but as long as that official is internally consistent, the teams will quickly and readily adjust to the official working the game. Vacillating in judgment and interpretation unduly disrupts the game and destroys the intent of athletic competition.

With differences between individuals unavoidable, how do players and coaches ever obtain the desired level of consistency in officiating? Although individual differences do exist, these effects are minimized by the use of correct rule interpretations. The rule interpretations applied uniformly by all officials lead to the high level of consistent officiating that enhances the athletic contest for players, coaches, fans and officials alike.

5. Decisiveness. Basketball officiating requires instantaneous judgmental decisions. In order to minimize the amount of controversy generated by these decisions, they must be made with the greatest degree of decisiveness possible. Each decision is always open to the "rose colored" interpretation of the players, coaches and fans; therefore, the good official will "sell" his call to the game participants. This selling process starts with a firm blast on the whistle, indicating to everyone that the official has seen an infraction of the rules and has deemed it necessary to rule on that infraction. A timid or too short of a blast on the whistle can lead to questioning by players and coaches and sometimes may not be heard at all, leading to confusion on the part of the players, coaches, and fans and presenting problems if not heard by the fellow official. This call can determine whether or not baskets count, personal fouls are recorded or even if technical fouls are to be assessed. Second, and often as important as the whistle in a hotly contested game with a great deal of crowd noise, is the hand signal. The proper open or closed hand signal must be given *immediately* following the whistle blast. In a crowded gymnasium this may be the only notification available to the timer that an infraction has occurred. Finally, the proper hand signal must be given to insure that everyone is aware of the type of infraction.

Controversial calls are always subject to criticism. However, the call that is made decisively minimizes the controversy. Basketball officials are required to make a large number of quick decisions in each game. These decisions should be made in a way that will leave no question in the minds of players, coaches, or fans as to the correctness of that decision. In general, the more potential for question, the greater the degree of decisiveness required.

6. Confidence. Confidence and decisiveness are closely related. Confidence deals more with the attitude of the official and the impression he makes on fans, players, and coaches; while decisiveness is concentrated on the mechanics of officiating. Anxiety and self-doubt have no place in the mind of the good official. When mentally preparing to work a basketball game, the official must be absolutely confident of his ability to maintain control of the game. This is often a problem with younger officials as they work their way toward officiating varsity games. The feeling that, "Maybe I've moved up the ladder too fast" or, "Maybe I'm not ready for the speed and the size of varsity players" frequently enters the mind of the new official. If those feelings prevail, that official is not ready and has moved up too fast.

Confidence is gained through experience and knowledge of the game. The confident official is aware of all the possible situations that can arise and he is prepared with the correct response. He is also aware that should a completely unique situation present itself, he will be able to call upon his knowledge of the rules and their intent to make a fair and honest judgment. Confidence is reflected in the attitude, voice projection and game control of every good official.

7. Fairness. Some call it honesty and some call it integrity, but uppermost in the mind of all officials has to be fairness. The intent of the official is to equally apply a set of pre-designated rules to both teams so that neither team is placed at a disadvantage. This can only be accomplished through complete fairness. Fairness has many enemies. The good official must be aware of all the possible areas in which fairness can be compromised. Externally, the players constantly try to take advantage of the rules through personal fouls, violations, etc. Coaches also operate in a manner constantly bordering on unfairness. Illegal substitutions and time-outs are two seen most often. External forces affecting fairness are clearly covered in the rules and are dealt with very effectively by the vast majority of officials. Internal factors are much more difficult to deal with. The official must constantly guard against permitting the coaches' constant questioning of each call to influence the next and all subsequent calls. Coaches constantly attempt to intimidate an official through verbal abuse and crowd-inciting gestures. The good official should either control this action through application of bench decorum rules or completely ignore these attempts at influence. In either case, the official must objectively view each situation independent of the effect on the crowd, players or game.

8. Courage. In order to implement all those qualities required of the great official, he must possess a great deal of courage. Officials are often referred to in the same breath as the opponent and generally are not liked by either team. This is most unfortunate, because they are as necessary to the game as either team, both coaches, and all the fans. Courageous officials must make decisions without regard for the score, its effect on the players, fans, coaches or game, and independent from all the pressures applied both internally and externally. The courageous official must place fairness above all else and strive to "call them as he sees them." The ability to resist pressure and intimidation determine the reputation of the official. Honest, fair officiating is appreciated by all involved and is rewarded in the long run.

9. Hustle. There is no excuse for not hustling. Hustling requires no knowledge of the rules, courage, or any of the other prerequisites. It only requires motivation and dedication on the part of the official. Hustle will improve your ability to demonstrate those other qualities needed for good officiating. Hustle will enable you to be in the proper position to execute good judgment. You can't make good judgment calls unless you can properly see the play. Hustle will also improve your consistency. It will enable you to get to the same spot each time to see the same play from the same angle and hopefully make the same call. Being consistent means being fair; therefore, hustle improves your fairness. Hustle also will improve your confidence by permitting you to be in control of each situation. By hustling, the fast break will not go by you and make you call it from behind, but rather place you out in front where the entire scene of action can be seen clearly. Hustle even helps you maintain your level of physical fitness.

Hustle is an attribute admired and respected by coaches, players, and fans. It is what the coach tries to instill in his players. In any athletic contest both the players and coaches are working as hard as they possibly can, and they deserve an official who is working as hard as they are. Hustle includes mental readiness, physical movement and a genuine interest in the game. Care must be taken to avoid the two extremes—pointless running to give the impression of the hustle and the "rocking chair" official who calls the entire game from the same spot.

10. Poise. Basketball games are often played at a very high emotional pitch. These emotions are stimulated in the tension of the players, the anxiety of the coach, and the excitement of the fans. Amid the chaos, the official must stand as the steadying force. The official exhibits his confidence and poise by remaining the one area of strict control in an arena filled with confusion. Maintaining control requires a great deal of concentration on the part of the good official. He must be able to withstand the irate coach and endure the endless taunts of the losing hometown crowd.

During the game action, the official has several different opportunities to keep the emotional level of the contest at a level where it does not interfere with the outcome of the game. When administering a throw-in, a slow and deliberate action can restore order to the game. A gentle pause on the free-throw line to insure that all players and the other official are properly lined up helps return calmness to the game and may even relieve tensions built up in the free thrower. Another way to exhibit poise is the method of calling violations and fouls. After blowing the whistle and raising the appropriate hand signal, don't hurry. You have the attention of everyone in the gymnasium, and they all must wait for you to tell them what has happened. Be deliberate. Plan exactly what your next move will be and give the proper signal. In reporting the foul to the scorer—hustle, but don't hurry, to a spot sufficiently close to the scorer's table where you can be heard, and then slowly and calmly give the scorer the number and color of the player who has committed the foul. Your voice should be steady and firm. It is imperative that some situations be handled with poise. Ejection of players or coaches for unsportsmanlike conduct is probably the most critical of these situations. These should be handled in a manner that conveys the message "You have left me no alternative; I'm sorry, but I'll have to remove you from the game." Never let the ejection take on the form of revenge.

Poise is complete self-control and is not always the easiest thing to maintain. However, it is essential to the good official. The expression, "A soft answer turneth away wrath," should be kept in the mind of the official at all times under all circumstances.

Don'ts for Officials

Good basketball officials face many pitfalls that can hamper the maximum development of officiating skills. The following is a list of areas of potential conflict for the official. Care should be taken to avoid all of these "don'ts."

1. Don't be over-sensitive. The official with "rabbit ears" should leave the game. Remember that every call made in the game will have one-half of the people agreeing with you and the other half disagreeing. This situation leads to verbal abuse. This must be ignored, whether it is by players, fans, or coaches. A good rule to follow is "Don't embarrass me, and I won't embarrass you."

2. Don't show off. The intent of the athletic contest is not to be a showcase for the officials' talents. The attraction is the two teams. The official should only be a mediating force between the two teams to insure fair and equal competition. The good official remains in the background until the action summons him to the forefront; he performs his duties, and then returns to obscurity.

3. Don't argue with coaches, players, or fans. Becoming involved in a heated debate with one of the participants serves no useful purpose to either party. In the majority of cases, your decision has already been made and will not be changed by any amount of discussion. A short explanation of what you saw and of the call should be the extent of any conversation. The game should be resumed as soon possible. After the game is over and a coach persists in his demands for an explanation, do so in a brief, courteous manner. Do not try to win him over to your point of view. One of the best ways to end this type of conversation is with three words, "in my judgment."

4. Don't anticipate. The good official will never assume something is going to happen. Just because the next thing that should happen looks likely, there are no guarantees. Let the play dictate your calls. You must not act, but rather react to the various play situations. Anticipations lead to inadvertent whistles and decreases the credibility of both members of the officiating team.

5. Don't criticize your partner. In any basketball game there are three teams involved: The two teams playing the game and the team of officials working the game. In many situations the official has only one true ally on the court—the other official. The good official remembers that all his calls reflect on his partner and that all his partner's calls reflect on him. The relationship must be one of mutual support.

6. Don't fraternize with participants. An official's integrity must always remain above question. The visiting of hospitality rooms should be avoided. Regardless of what the discussion entailed, misconceptions can result. All contact with players, coaches, or fans should be on a strictly professional level.

7. Don't be irresponsible. The good official accepts all game assignments without regard to the teams involved (unless a conflict of interest arises), distance traveled, or calibur of play. Contracts between the official and the assignment secretary or individual school should, whenever possible, be in writing. Be as businesslike as possible when handling correspondence regarding officiating.

After accepting a contract to work a game, the official should make every attempt to honor that contract. The official should make every attempt to anticipate problems regarding travel. Adverse weather or traffic conditions may require the official to leave earlier than originally planned. If, for some reason, the official is unable to honor a contract, he should contact the assignment secretary or school administration and explain the situation

17

honestly. Under no circumstances should an official cancel one contract in order to accept another.

8. Don't drink alcoholic beverages. You, as an independent contractor, have assumed the responsibility of officiating a game to the best of your ability. An overindulgence in alcoholic beverages will surely impair your ability to perform to your maximum. One pre-game drink may have little affect on you physiologically, but if detected, it is sure to affect both the players and coaches psychologically. If the game begins with participants doubting your ability, the situation will surely not improve.

9. Don't come unprepared. Being prepared to officiate a basketball game includes several different types of preparation. First, you must be in good physical condition to minimize the effects of fatigue. Second, you must be prepared in your appearance. The uniform should be clean, neat and in accordance with accepted standards. Personal grooming should also lend itself to the atmosphere. Finally, the good official should be mentally prepared. Mental preparation includes knowledge of the rules, knowledge of the teams, whenever possible, and concentration on the task at hand.

10. Don't get emotionally involved. The official must remain the one area in which emotions are always completely under control. The official cannot let verbal abuse, excitement of the crowd, or the game situation enter his mind and affect his abilities. Uncontrolled emotions should not be allowed to determine the outcome of a game, and it is the official's responsibility to maintain his personal emotional control.

Uniform and Equipment

The standard uniform will vary somewhat from association to association; however, there are basic rules to be followed. A standard black and white vertically striped knit shirt, with a collar is accepted everywhere. Normally, the shirt has a zipper partially down the front. Most associations prefer that the shirt does not have a pocket on the front or black mesh inserts sewn into the area of the armpit. Turtle-neck shirts are unacceptable. Black, straight-legged trousers, all black shoes with black laces, black socks, and a black belt should be worn with the striped shirt. All of the above items should be neat and clean for each game assignment. Some officials also choose to wear a solid black nylon jacket. This is optional, but care should be taken to insure that the two officials working together give off the appearance of being a team.

Two types of whistles are currently popular with basketball officials. When blown, each should emit a sound that can be heard above the ordinary sounds of a basketball game. The metal whistle is generally worn with a white rubber mouth guard to protect the teeth. The black plastic whistle normally does not require the rubber guard. The type of whistle used is a personal preference of the official. The whistle, regardless of type, is secured around the neck by a black lanyard. Each official should carry a second whistle in case of emergency. It is a good idea to start each new season with two new whistles. Whistles used and left in storage during the "off season" are not completely reliable. The "pea" inside the whistle dries out and will break under pressure.

It is important that the uniform present a pleasant, neat appearance because it is the first impression you will make on the participants of the game.

Summary

Good basketball officiating has ten basic prerequisites: 1. knowledge of the rules (intent included), 2. physical fitness, 3. good judgment, 4. consistency, 5. decisiveness, 6. confidence, 7. fairness, 8, courage, 9. hustle, and 10. poise. The official desiring to advance in the officiating avocation should make special efforts to concentrate on developing these characteristics. If evaluations are used in the local association, the official should keep his own record of progress. Concentrate on those areas of weakness, while maintaining the remainder of the characteristics at the highest level.

Officiating also presents some possibilities for conflict for the official. Officials must be careful not to be too sensitive to the neverending stream of verbal abuse from players, coaches and fans. They must also place their job in the proper perspective to the game itself. "Showboating" and power struggles with coaches are not conducive to good game control. The official must also maintain complete self-control by conducting himself in a professional manner at all times and coming to each contest both mentally and physically prepared.

Local variations in the proper uniform are slight. The standard black and white vertically striped knit shirt with all black accessories (slacks, shoes, socks and belt) is accepted almost everywhere. Two functioning whistles should be carried at all times. It is important that the uniform and personal grooming habits of the official present a neat, clean appearance for all games worked.

Hustle is one of the most important attributes of a good official.

CHAPTER II

Procedures For Officiating Basketball

The game of basketball is officiated by a team of two officials: a referee and an umpire. Each of these officials has specific duties to perform. This chapter will cover pre-game duties, duties during game situations, and post-game duties for each of the officials.

Duties of the Officials

Referee: The referee is the ultimate judge in all situations, but he does not have the power to overrule decisions made by the umpire.

Umpire: The umpire shall work as an equal partner to the referee within the duties assigned to him by the rules.

Pre-game Procedures

Officials should arrive in advance of game time and immediately notify the home management of their arrival. This early arrival accomplishes two things. First, it will place at ease the mind of the home team administration that the officials are available and will be ready to work the game as scheduled. Secondly, and more important to the official, the early arrival gives the officiating team sufficient time to complete the pre-game conference. Prior to starting the actual pre-game conference, the referee should check the correct time and determine how much time can be spent on the pre-game discussion and still insure the officials' arrival on the court 30 minutes prior to game time. The pre-game conference is very important to the mental preparation of the official. It should, at a minimum, include the following:

1. Each official should make a thorough check of all his personal equipment. Check both whistles to insure that each is functioning properly. After checking the whistles, one should be used and the other should be carried as a spare for use in case of emergency.

2. A general review of responsibilities and proper mechanics should occupy the majority of the time spent in the pre-game conference. The review should cover any new rule changes, interpretations, and special rules. Discussion of these points helps each official become familiar with the manner in which the other will react to a particular situation. Rule changes are very important. This is especially true in areas where more than one local association is operating. Some minor differences in interpretation of rules may occur between associations. The differences should be resolved in the pre-game conference so that disagreements between the officials do not occur during the game. Remember, teamwork is important.

Specific game situations should be discussed. Court coverage is essential to good officiating. It may sound unimportant, but each situation (jump ball, throw-in, switching, foul shot, etc.) should be discussed from the point of view of both the lead and trail official. It is important that each official know what area he is covering and what area his partner is covering at all times. Switching, out-of-bounds, and simultaneous whistles are three examples of potential problems that can be avoided through the pre-game conference. Although strict mechanics dictate switching only on personal foul situations, some officials feel the flow of the game is improved by switching on specific violation situations. Knowing about this fact in advance could prevent both officials standing at the spot of the throw-in while the teams wait at the other end of the court. Out-of-bounds situations present another area of potential problems. The official administering the throw-in should be certain that his partner is ready and in position before presenting the ball to the player for the throw-in. A simple nod of the head from the lead official can be used to convey his readiness to his partner. Finally, simultaneous whistles on the part of both officials can be the most critical area of potential problems. Whether the team of officials uses a code whereby one official nods to the other, or some other system, both officials must be operating together when each makes a call simultaneously. It is extremely embarrassing, and a great deal of respect and credibility is lost when each official makes his separate call before checking what his partner has called. Also with the discussion of specific situations, each official should inform his partner of those particular plays or situations that present the biggest problem for him. An exchange of possible solutions can be beneficial to both officials.

3. Unusual situations or conditions specific to the team or gymnasium should be discussed last. Prior knowledge of the teams involved in the game

can be very helpful. If one of the teams is a "run and gun" team, review fast-break procedures; and if one of the teams is a "slow down" team, review the rules covering lack of sufficient action. Although it may not happen more than once in a season, the proper procedure for handling an injured player should be reviewed before each game worked. Finally, situations special to gymnasium or contest should be discussed. If the gymnasium floor is under-sized and/or has bleachers extending close to the boundary lines, restraining line procedures should be discussed. If a player, team, or coach has special characteristics, they should be noted.

The pre-game conference held in the officials' dressing room serves several purposes. It is a mental preparation for both officials. The conference allows both officials to rid their minds of extraneous influences and aids them in the concentration demanded by the game of basketball. Secondly, it is a review of all the reasonably possible situations that may confront them during the actual game. And finally, it is an exchange of ideas, insuring that each official is as familiar with the procedures of his partner as he can be. This familiarization enables the team of officials to present a consistent, fairly officiated game. Some members of the Southern California Basketball Officials Association use the following pre-game conference sheet as a reminding device to insure that all areas are covered during the pre-game conference. The sheet shows out-of-bounds responsibilities, court areas, and potential problem situations. The problem areas listed should be kept current with rule changes and rule interpretations. This list may also be personalized by the individual to reflect those areas most troublesome to him. It has proven to be a useful tool and, in the author's opinion, one that will aid in improving officiating whenever it is used.

After the pre-game conference and 30 minutes prior to the scheduled starting time, the two officials should enter the court together. The referee should inspect all equipment for safety and proper function. This inspection should include the court, ball, backboards, baskets, and timing and scoring devices. It is at this time that the referee designates the official timing device, the timer, the official scorebook, and the scorer. If all equipment is in proper working order, the referee briefs the official timer and scorer on their duties.

The official timer should be notified of the starting time, length of playing time, time-outs, overtimes, and the regulation hand signals to be used by the floor officials. In the event of a close game, the timer should be pre-warned that if the officials are unable to hear the timer's horn over the noise of the crowd, he (the timer) will be the final judge of whether a last-second shot will count or not. A pre-warned timer will assume this responsibility and assist the floor officials in making the correct decision. It is also the duty of the timer to notify the scorer ten minutes prior, and three minutes prior to the

DIAGRAM FOR PRE-GAME CONFERENCE

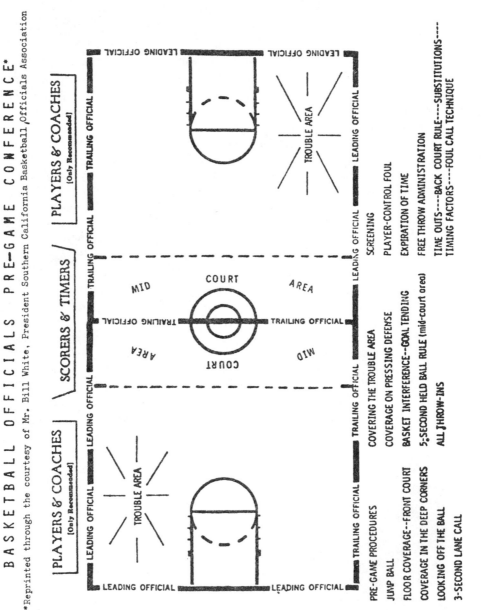

starting time and to notify the officials three minutes prior to starting time.

The official scorer should enter into the official scorebook the names, numbers, and starting players for each team. It is his duty to notify the referee if either team has failed to supply him with the above mentioned information. The official scorer normally works with at least one other non-official scorer. These two scorers should confer with each other after each entry into the official scorebook. It is the duty of the official scorer to notify the referee the moment any discrepancy arises. During the actual game, the official scorer is responsible for notifying the officials of the bonus rule, any player committing his fifth personal foul, excessive time-outs, illegal numbers, and illegal substitutions.

The total officiating team, including the official timer and scorer, must be a close-knit unit to properly officiate the athletic contest. Care should be taken by the referee to inform both the timer and scorer of *all* their duties in advance of the start of play and clarify any questions these two officials may have regarding their responsibilities. Good officiating requires teamwork. These two sideline officials may make the difference in a close game.

After completing the inspection of all equipment, including players' uniforms and equipment, and the assignment of the official timer and scorer have been made, the officials may continue with their pre-game responsibilities. Jurisdiction for the officials begins 30 minutes prior to game time. During this time, it is the responsibility of both officials to discuss any special conditions that may exist in the gymnasium, guard against violations of the dunking rule, and seek out the coaches of both teams. A pleasant self-introduction will aid in the human relations process that occurs during each game. Approximately 10 minutes prior to the start of the game, the umpire shall seek out the home captain and the referee shall seek out the visiting captain. The meeting with the captains should be held in the center restraining circle and should begin with the umpire introducing the home captain to the referee and vice versa. This meeting should be kept as brief as possible and should not include any attempts to outline rule interpretations. As the season progresses, the need for explanations and answering questions will decrease. During the meeting, the referee should inform both captains of the starting time, instruct the captains to have their players throw the ball to the nearest official after violations, and designate the color for each team. The meeting with the captains may include explanation of a particular ground rule pertaining to a point of interest, but brevity should be the overriding factor in this meeting. It is the captain's responsibility to convey to his coach and fellow players any explanation offered at the meeting. Actually, this is rarely necessary. If the referee feels there is a particular point in need of emphasis, it is recommended that the two officials mention this directly to the coaches. Preventing a confrontation before it happens is easier to handle than attempting to explain a situation to an already irate coach.

Normally, the final pre-game responsibility is to test the game ball. A properly inflated ball will rebound from the playing floor 49 to 54 inches when dropped from a height of 6 feet. Test-bounce the ball in several different areas to be certain that the variations are in the floor and not in the ball.

Game Procedures

With the completion of the pre-game procedures, the officials are now ready to begin the actual play of the game. The large majority of calls to be made during the game occurs in one of five major areas: jump-ball, out-of-bounds, full court press, time-out, and rule infractions. In each of these situations, it is necessary to use proper mechanics to insure good coverage at all times. The toss to begin the first and all subsequent periods shall be made by the referee. All other tosses occurring during play shall be made by the official facing the scorer's table at the time of the call. During all jump ball situations, the official making the toss should make the toss while facing the scorer's table. The other official should be near the sideline opposite the tossing official. The tossing official is responsible for a straight, high toss and all rule infractions committed by the two jumpers. When tossing the ball, the official should hold the whistle in his hand, not in his mouth. Damage to the teeth can easily occur if the whistle should be struck by an errant elbow of one of the jumpers. After the ball is tossed, the tossing official should remain in place until the area surrounding the circle is clear and it is safe to move into position. The "outside" official during the jump ball is primarily responsible for the eight non-jumpers. He should be looking for fouls and violations of the restraining circle. It is also the responsibility of this official to blow a bad toss dead. The tossing official will not have his whistle in his mouth and, although he may be the first to realize a bad toss, the "outside" official must make the call. After the ball is tossed, the non-tossing official goes with the direction of the ball and becomes the lead official. The tossing official becomes the trail official as soon as the area around the circle has cleared and he is able to make his way into position.

All jump balls occur at the circle closest to which the held ball was called except in the following situations: 1. At the beginning of each period or extra period, the jump shall start at the center circle. 2. Following a double foul in which no free throws are awarded, the jump will be at the center circle. 3. Following a false double foul in which free throws are awarded, the jump ball will be at the center circle.

Whether calling the ball out-of-bounds or a violation, the out-of-bounds situation requires five basic mechanics of the official: 1. Blow the whistle long and loud enough to insure all the participants and the other official are aware that a call has been made. 2. Raise the hand and signal time out. 3. Signal the type of violation. 4. Call out in a strong, sure voice the color of the team to which the ball will be awarded and indicate the direction this team will travel. 5. Indicate the spot at which the throw-in will take place.

In calling the out-of-bounds situation, the lead official is responsible for the endline and sideline to his immediate left and the trail official is responsible for the division line and the sideline to his left. Each official should respect the territory of his partner and strive not to make out-of-bounds calls in his partner's area. If a ball goes out at, or very near, the intersection of the two territories, the likelihood that both officials will blow their whistles is high. In this case, the two officials should use whatever system was decided upon in the pre-game conference. Usually eye-to-eye contact is established and a word or nod from one official indicating who will take the call is sufficient. The referee can be pre-designated to decide which official will make the call. The system will establish a clear routine and will avoid any unnecessary delays in making the proper call. A second problem sometimes arises with regard to the out-of-bounds call. The responsibility for the ball going out of bounds in a certain area is very clear; however, the official in that area may not be absolutely certain which team caused the ball to go out of bounds. He may have been screened out, or for some other reason was unable to see the play. It is still his responsibility to blow the whistle, but he must look to his partner for help. Eye-to-eye contact is again essential. Some officials prefer a small, undetectable signal; but to avoid all chances of confusion and insure the proper call, the outside official should clearly indicate or announce the direction or color of the team to be awarded the ball. The official who was unable to see the play should not feel the need to apologize as long as the reason was legitimate and unavoidable.

After the out-of-bounds violation has been established, a throw-in must follow. A spot on the floor and one player from the team should be designated by the nearest official to administer the throw-in. Both officials should use the "boxing in" principle on all throw-ins. This principle states that the player making the throw-in and the majority of the remaining players should be kept between the two officials. In this way, the floor and all the action are given the best possible coverage. After the positioning of both officials to insure the play is "boxed" and there is no confusion on the part of the players, the administering official should hand the ball to the designated player. It is never proper to toss the ball to the player. After handing the ball to the designated player, the official should take a step back to allow the player sufficient room to execute the throw-in. The official should use a visible hand count.

Throw-ins in the front court may be handled by either official, depending on where the ball went out or the spot of the violation, but the trail official is responsible for all throw-ins in the back court area.

The full court press presents several unique problems for the officials. Most obviously is the fact that the area needed to be covered by the two officials is doubled. In all the other situations, action is concentrated in one-half of the area of the total court; but, in the full court press situation, the entire court from endline to endline needs to be covered. The additional pressure for coverage is greater on the lead official than on the trail official. The lead official must remain in the back court area to assist the trail official with the coverage of the major action area. The problem comes with the high potential for a long pass. The lead official must be constantly alert for this pass and be prepared to get into position along the front court baseline as soon as this long pass takes place. It is almost required that the lead official be in two places faster than the ball can travel from one to another. If no long pass occurs, the lead and the trail official move down the floor according to the speed and location of the action. In some situations, the officials may be positioned directly opposite each other. The full court press also tends to speed up the action and forces teams to play with less control. The maintenance of game control should be carefully watched during full court pressing.

The time-out would seem to be a relatively simple situation, but it, too, can lead to trouble if not handled properly. The official making the call should blow a long, loud whistle and raise his hand to signal the time-out. The calling official should then proceed toward the scorer's bench and inform the scorer which team requested the time-out. This procedure eliminates any problems in miscommunications from the calling official to the other official to the scorer. The free official (non-calling) should retrieve the ball and then position himself near the spot where the ball will be put into play. The positioning of the free official near the spot of the impending throw-in avoids any confusion by the two teams. The calling official remains in the area of the scorer's bench until the time-out has expired. During this period, he is available to recognize any substitutions and provide any information requested by the off-floor officials and coaches. If all time-out situations are handled consistently in the manner described, the officiating team will be able to avoid many problems.

The final game situation to be discussed is the calling of fouls, which holds the greatest potential for problems. The player does not believe he committed a foul, the coach does not believe the player committed the foul, and neither do the fans. On any given call, but especially foul calls, approximately one-half of the participants in any game feel it was incorrectly called. Proper game procedures can help decrease this number, although it certainly will never reach zero. Decisiveness and confidence play a large part in calling fouls. The whistle blast must be long, loud, and accompanied by a raised, clenched fist. These actions will, both, stop the clock and indicate that a foul has been committed. The calling official should move toward the fouling player, extending the opposite hand, palm down and fingers extended, toward the fouler's midsection. He should verbally inform the fouler by number that he had committed the foul. Be sure the fouling player is aware that he has fouled. At this time, the calling official should also make a mental note of the player fouled. In the case of awarded free-throws, it is essential that the officials know which player on the offended team should be awarded the free-throws. The calling official should then move toward the scorer's table to a position close enough to be heard clearly by the official scorer. The proper signal for the foul should be given and the color and number of the fouling player should be verbally stated, as well as the number of free-throws to be attempted.

The free official should immediately freeze upon hearing his partner's whistle. While the calling official is following the above-mentioned procedure, the free official should maintain vigilance over the entire scene to handle any extraneous action. Only after he is certain that all action has ceased should the official retrieve the loose ball and, if free-throws are to be awarded, arrange the teams in proper position along the free-throw lane. He should position himself under the basket facing down court. From this position, he will be able to recognize substitutes and check for the bonus free-throw indicator when the calling official's back is to the scorer's table.

Several different foul situations require special mechanics. If a player control foul has been called, the procedure is identical with one exception. Instead of indicating the number of free-throws awarded, the official signals a player control foul. The free official should retrieve the ball and move directly to the out-of-bounds spot nearest the spot of the foul. If the foul call necessitates a switch, the free official hands the ball to the calling official when he returns from the scorer's table and then quickly proceeds to his proper position for the throw-in. If the switch has already been made, he retains the ball at the spot of the throw-in until the other official is in position and signals he is ready for play. He then hands the ball to the player for the throw-in, steps back, and begins the visible 5 second count.

Technical fouls, double fouls, and false double fouls follow the basic procedures for personal fouls with some minor modifications. The technical foul presents problems because it is a very emotional situation that normally occurs only when the officials must reassert their control of the game and its participants. The calling official follows the same procedure as for the personal foul except the signal is changed to the technical foul "T". The free official retrieves the ball, keeps the players away from the free-throw area, and hands the ball to his fellow official when he returns from the scorer's table. The free official proceeds to the midcourt area and is ready to put the ball in play when the free-throw is completed. It is recommended that the official go to the midcourt area on the sideline opposite the player's benches. In this way, possible confrontations with the coach of the team involved are avoided.

If a double foul occurs, the calling official proceeds as indicated; but the free official, after retrieving the ball, goes to the center circle and lines the teams up for the jump ball. If the foul was a false double foul, the two officials perform their respective duties as demanded by the personal foul and then separate. One official proceeds to each end of the court to the area of the free-throw line. The first official completing the free-throw then rolls the ball to the opposite official and proceeds to position himself at the center circle ready to administer the jump ball which follows.

Post-game Procedures

The sounding of the final horn does not terminate the responsibilities of the officials. The referee should proceed to the scorer's table and approve the final score in the official scorebook. This approval ends the jurisdiction of the officials. The free official should retrieve the ball unless some prior arrangements have been made. The officials should leave the floor together as quickly as possible. Any discussion with either coach, players, or fans is neither feasible nor professional. The game has already been decided and discussion will not alter the outcome. Away from the noise and confusion of the court, both officials should recount any particular situation that caused problems. This is a time for professional growth, and advice from fellow officials should not be taken as personal criticism.

Floor Coverage

A final brief note on floor coverage is needed. It is critical that all parts of the floor are covered by at least one official at all times. This is most easily accomplished by dividing the area to be covered with a line perpendicular to a line drawn from one official to the other. This line should always divide the area approximately equal. This division is not designed to place any restrictions on the area of jurisdiction. Either official is able to call any infraction he sees. It is possible that the closest official will fail to see an infraction; and, rather than permit it to go undetected, most officials prefer to have it called by the second official. Under the normal half court area coverage, the area around the free-throw lane, extending as far out as the top of the circle, is an area in which the responsibilities for calling rule infractions rests equally on both officials. This area is where the predominance of the action takes place and must be monitored by both officials. In the case of simultaneous whistles in this area, each official should acknowledge the other before making any indication of the call.

Court coverage and the subsequent proper positioning of the officials allow the two men to cover the court with maximum efficiency. Each official should be aware of the position of his partner at all times. The official who is "away" from the action should adjust his position according to the necessary movements of the other official. The court division and overlapping areas of coverage make up a dynamic system of coverage. It allows the officials to constantly change their areas of responsibility to adjust to the play while maintaining thorough and efficient coverage of all the court surface.

Summary

The two, or sometimes three, officials assigned to work a basketball game are given the title of referee and umpire only for the separation of the duty. They must work equally as a team to give the game its proper guidance and control.

Pre-game procedures and, especially, the dressing room conference provide the opportunity for two separate individuals to exchange ideas. This exchange and familiarization period will allow these two officials, who may well be meeting for the first time, the opportunity to mesh their differences and ideas into a cohesive unit of officiating efficiency. The pre-game conference sheet is used to remind the officials of all the possible problem areas they may encounter while working the upcoming game. This device may be personalized to fit the needs of the individual official.

On the floor, pre-game procedures should be followed to insure that all the preliminaries to the contest are completed and that nothing is overlooked. A critical portion of the pre-game procedures is the assignment of the official timer and the official scorer. These two off-floor officials are as much a part of the officiating team as are the referee and the umpire. Their contributions to the successful management of the game are not as dramatic or as visible as are the on-floor officials', but never less important.

Game procedures are important, whether the situation concerns a jump ball, out-of-bounds, full court press, time-out, or foul. It is critical that proper mechanics be followed to present consistency throughout the contest. Mechanics are the basics that result in consistent and fair officiating.

Post-game procedures should only consist of the referee's approval of the final score, an orderly exit from the floor, and a discussion of problem situations that may have arisen during the game.

CHAPTER III

Basketball Signals

Basketball hand signals are the official's way of informing everyone in the gymnasium of what has happened on court. It would be impossible to verbally communicate with the fan seated in the highest row or even with the first row during the abundance of crowd noise that accompanies a basketball game. The signals are a consistent way of explaining why a particular action has taken place. When the official properly executes these signals, they permit everyone to participate totally in the action.

The most critical signal, when any infraction occurs, is the raising of the hand to the fullest extension of the arm. Whether the hand is open indicating violation, or closed indicating foul, this arm-raising action should occur immediately following the official's whistle. This action informs the timer to stop the clock and alerts the scorer that information will follow. Once this action is completed, the official should proceed with the explaining signal in a deliberate, controlled manner. This insures clarity and aids the official in his control of the game.

The following illustrations are the hand signals most frequently used in officiating basketball. It is confusing and unprofessional to use variations or self-invented signals. Consistent use of accepted signals eliminates confusion and aids in the enjoyment of the game by everyone.

RECOMMENDED BASKETBALL SIGNALS

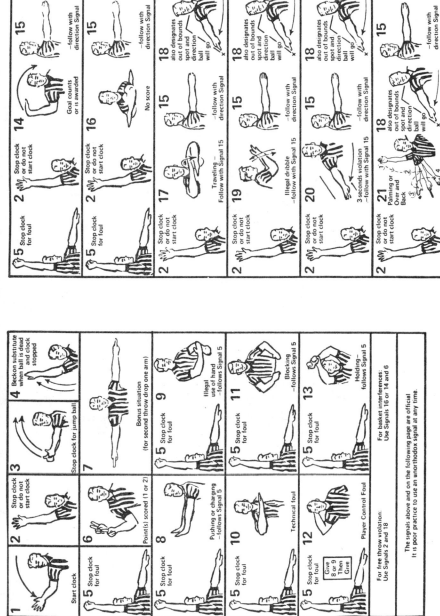

1. Start clock
2. Stop clock for foul
3. Stop clock or do not start clock
4. Beckon substitute when ball is dead and clock stopped
5. Stop clock for jump ball
6. Point(s) scored (1 or 2)
7. Bonus situation (for second throw drop one arm)
8. Stop clock for foul
9. Illegal use of hand —follows Signal 5
10. Pushing or charging —follows Signal 5
11. Stop clock for foul / Blocking —follows Signal 5
12. Stop clock for foul / Technical foul
13. Stop clock for foul / Holding—follows Signal 5

Player Control Foul
Give 8 or 9 Then Give

For free throw violation: Use Signals 2 and 18
For basket interferences: Use Signals 16 or 14 and 6

The signals above and on the following page are official
It is poor practice to use an unorthodox signal at any time.

1. Stop clock for foul / 2. Stop clock or do not start clock / 14. Goal counts or is awarded / 15. —follow with direction Signal
2. Stop clock for foul / 2. Stop clock or do not start clock / 16. No score / 15. —follow with direction Signal
3. Stop clock or do not start clock / 17. Traveling— Follow with Signal 15 / 15. —follow with direction Signal / 18. also designates out of bounds spot and direction ball will go
4. Stop clock or do not start clock / 19. Illegal dribble —follow with Signal 15 / 15. —follow with direction Signal / 18. also designates out of bounds spot and direction ball will go
5. Stop clock or do not start clock / 20. 3-seconds violation —follow with Signal 15 / 15. —follow with direction Signal / 18. also designates out of bounds spot and direction ball will go
6. Stop clock or do not start clock / 21. Palming or Over and Back / 18. also designates out of bounds spot and direction ball will go / 15. —follow with direction Signal

33

CHAPTER IV

Rules

The first set of rules for the game of basketball were written in 1891 and contained thirteen original rules. Since that time there have been numerous rule changes. Even today each year brings rule changes and new interpretations of old rules. The rules presented in this chapter are those used by the National Basketball Association (NBA). For the reader's benefit, the major rule differences between the NBA rules and the rules of both the National High School Federation and the National College Athletic Association (NCAA) are listed immediately following each rule section.

Each level of basketball operates under a set of rules distinct to that level of play. It is essential for the official working more than one level of play to remember the differences and have them clearly in mind at all times.

Official Rules

RULE NO. 1—COURT DIMENSIONS—EQUIPMENT

Section I—Court Dimensions

a. The playing court shall be measured and marked as shown in court diagram. (See page 4)

b. A free throw lane shall be marked at each end of the court with dimensions and markings as shown on court diagram. All boundary lines are part of the lane; lane space marks and neutral zone marks are **not**. The color of the lane space marks and neutral zones shall contrast with the color of the boundary lines. The areas identified by the lane space markings are two inches by thirty-six and the neutral zone marks are twelve inches by thirty-six inches.

c. A free throw line, 2 inches wide, shall be drawn across each of the circles indicated in court diagram. It shall be parallel to the end line and shall be 15 feet from the plane of the face of the backboard.

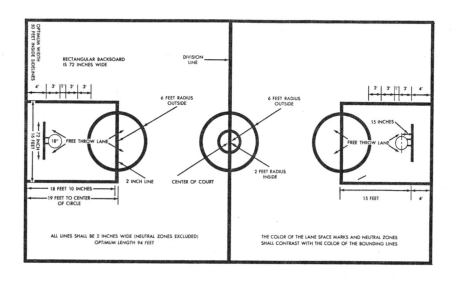

Section II—Equipment

a. The backboard shall be a rectangle measuring 6 feet horizontally and 4 feet vertically. The front surface shall be flat and unless it is transparent, the color shall be white.

b. If the backboard is transparent, it shall be marked as follows: a rectangle marked by a 2″ white line shall be centered behind the ring. This rectangle shall have outside dimensions of 24″ horizontally and 18″ vertically. (On a non-transparent board, the rectangle target should be bright orange in color. Borders of the backboard shall be marked with a white line 3″ in width.

NOTE: Home management is required to have a spare board on hand for emergencies, and a steel tape or extension ruler and a level for use if necessary.

c. Each basket shall consist of a metal ring 18″ in inside diameter with white cord net 15 to 18 inches in length. The cord of the net shall not be less than 30 thread nor more than 120 thread and shall be constructed as to check the ball momentarily as it passes through the basket.

d. Each basket ring shall be securely attached to the backboard with its upper edge 10 feet above and parallel to the floor and equidistant from the vertical edges of the board. The nearest point of the inside edge of the ring shall be 6″ from the plane of the face of the board. The ring shall be painted orange.

e. (1) The ball shall be an officially approved NBA ball.

   (2) Six balls must be made available to each team for pre-game warmup.

---

1. Federation—Court dimensions of 50′ × 84′ or less.
   NCAA   —Court dimensions of 50′ × 94′ or less.
   NBA   —Court dimensions of 50′ × 94′ required.
2. Federation—Fan-shaped backboard preferred.
   NCAA   —Rectangular backboard required.
   NBA   —Rectangular backboard required.
3. Federation—Free throw lane is 12′ wide.
   NCAA   —Free throw lane is 12′ wide.
   NBA   —Free throw lane is 16′ wide.

Rules

RULE NO. 2— OFFICIALS AND THEIR DUTIES

Section I— The Officials

a. The officials shall be three referees, assisted by two trained timers, one to operate the game clock, the other to operate the 24 second timer and by a scorer who will compile the statistics of the game. All officials shall be approved by the Commissioner.

b. The referees shall wear the uniform prescribed by the NBA.

Section II— Duties of the Referees

a. A referee shall, prior to start of game, inspect and approve all equipment, including court, baskets, balls, backboards, timers and scorer's equipment.

b. He shall not permit any player to wear braces or protective equipment without padding protection which, in his judgment, is dangerous to other players.

c. The referee must check the three game balls to see they are properly inflated to a pressure between 7½ and 8½ pounds, if necessary.

d. The senior official shall be the referee in charge.

e. Both officials shall be at the scorer's table 5 minutes before game time. They will at that time go over scoring and timing procedures with table personnel.

NOTE: If a coach desires to discuss a rule or interpretation of a rule prior to the start of a game, it will be mandatory for the officials to ask the other coach to be present during the discussion. The same procedure shall be followed for requests made at the start of a period.

f. The referee shall toss the ball at the start of the game; he shall decide whether or not a goal shall count if the officials disagree; he shall decide matters upon which scorers and timers disagree.

g. One official shall be present during the pre-game warm-up period to observe and report to the Commissioner any infractions of Rule 12-VII i— hanging on the rim. During the playoffs the third official shall be assigned to this duty.

Section III— Elastic Power

The referees shall have power to make decisions on any point not specifically covered in the rules. The Commissioner will be advised of all such decisions at the earliest possible moment.

Section IV— Different Decisions By Officials

The senior official shall have the authority to set aside or question decisions made by the other within the limits of his respective outlined duties.

QUESTION (1)— A violation and personal contact occur at the same time. Both are observed by the same official, or the violation by one and foul by the other. What is the proper procedure?

ANSWER— The foul takes precedence over any violation.

QUESTION (2)— Ball in flight on try for field goal by A1, A2 pushes B1. After personal foul while ball is rolling around the ring B2 bats ball away from ring. Which infraction of the rules shall be penalized?

ANSWER— Both. Two points to Team A, the penalty for personal foul.

NOTE: It is the primary duty of the trial official to signal if goals count. If for any reason he does not know if goal is made he should ask the other official. If neither saw the goal made they should refer to the timer. If the timer saw the goal scored it shall count. Exception: The drive-in or quick down court shot shall be the primary responsibility of the lead official.

Rules

Section V — Time and Place for Decisions

a. The officials shall have power to have decisions for infractions of rules committed either within or outside the boundary lines. This includes periods when the game may be stopped for any reason.

b. When a foul occurs, an official shall signal the timer to stop his watch and if it is a personal foul, he shall also designate the number of the offender to the scorer and indicate with his fingers the number of free throws to be attempted.

c. When a team is entitled to a throw-in, an official shall clearly signal the act which caused the ball to become dead, the throw-in spot and the team entitled to the throw-in; unless it follows a successful goal or an awarded goal.

Section VI — Correcting Errors

a. Officials may correct an error if a rule is inadvertently set aside and results in:

(1) A team not shooting a merited penalty shot.

(2) A team shooting an unmerited penalty shot.

(3) Permitting the wrong player to attempt a free throw.

NOTE: Officials should be notified of error at first dead ball. All errors must be rectified before the start of the next quarter. Ball is not in play on corrected foul and whether foul shot is made or missed, play shall be resumed at the same spot where referee declared the ball dead and under the same conditions as would have prevailed had play not been stopped to correct error. If the officials are notified of error within 24 seconds, any play action that occurs during that time period is to be nullified. This nullifies scoring and fouls committed by either team. However, if a player or coach is ejected during this period he is not permitted to return to the game. The referee shall also reset the game clock so that the time left to play shall be the same as it was when the error occurred. However, any acts of unsportsmanlike conduct or points scored therefrom are not nullified.

NOTE: Errors in the fourth quarter and over-times, in order to be rectified, must be discovered before the end of the period.

Section VII — Duties of Scorers

a. The scorers shall record the field goals made, the free throws made and missed, and shall keep a running summary of the points scored. They shall record the personal and technical fouls called on each player and shall notify the referee immediately when a sixth personal foul is called on any player. They shall record the time-outs charged to each team, shall notify a team and its coach through an official whenever that team takes a sixth and seventh charged time-out and shall notify the nearest official each time a team is granted a charged time-out in excess of the legal number. In case there is a question about an error in the scoring, the scorer shall check with the referee at once to find the discrepancy. If the error cannot be found, the referee shall accept the record of the official scorer, unless he has knowledge that forces him to decide otherwise.

b. The scorers shall keep a record of the names, numbers and positions of players who are to start the game and of all substitutes who enter the game. When there is an infraction of the rules pertaining to submission of line-up, substitutions or numbers of players, they shall notify the nearer official immediately if the ball is dead, or as soon as it becomes dead if it is in play when the infraction is discovered. Scorer shall mark the time at which players are disqualified by reason of recieving six personal fouls so that it may be easy to ascertain the order in which the players are eligible to go back in the game in accordance with Rule 3-1.

c. The scorers shall use a horn or other device unlike that used by the officials or timers to signal the officials. This may be used when the ball is dead or in certain specified situations when the ball is in control of a given team. Scorer shall signal coach on the bench on every personal foul, designating number of personal fouls a player has, and number of team. NOTE: White paddles—team fouls; Red paddles—personal fouls.

d. When a player is disqualified from the game, or whenever a penalty shot is being awarded, a buzzer, a siren or some other clear audible sound must be used by the scorer or timer to notify the game officials. It is the duty of the scorekeeper to be certain the officials have acknowledged the 6th personal foul buzzer and the penalty shot buzzer.

QUESTION (1)—The scorers fail to notify the official that a player has commited his 6th personal foul and he remains in the game. What should be done?

ANSWER—Playing time consumed, if any, and points scored count. The offending player must be removed as soon as the official discovers the error. Scorers should notify an official as soon as a player commits his 6th personal foul, but if play is resumed before such notification, they should signal when the ball is next dead or is in control of the offending team.

QUESTION (2)—What should be done if the scorer's horn sounds, while the ball is in play?

ANSWER—Players should ignore the horn since it does not make the ball dead. The scorers should not signal while the ball is in play except in certain cases such as are noted in the first question above. The officials must use their judgment in blowing the ball dead to consult the scorers.

QUESTION (3)—If the scorers fail to notify a team or its coach when it takes its 7th charged time-out, should the team be penalized if it takes an 8th time-out?

ANSWER—Yes.

e. Scorers shall record on scoreboard the number of team fouls to a total of five—which will indicate that the team is in a penalty situation.

Section VIII—Duties of Timers

a. The timers shall note when each half is to start and shall notify the referee and coach five minutes before this time, or cause them to be notified at least five minutes before the half is to start. They shall signal the scorers two minutes before starting time. They shall record playing time and time of stoppages as provided in the rules. The timer shall be provided with an extra stop watch to be used in time outs, etc. other than the official game clock or watch. Official clock or scoreboard should show 12 minute quarters.

b. At the beginning of each quarter or extra period or whenever play is resumed by a jump ball the game clock shall be started when the ball has been legally tapped by either of the jumpers. If, after time has been out, the ball is put in play by a throw-in from out of bounds or by a free throw, the game watch shall be started when the official gives the time-in signal as the ball is touched by a player in the court.

c. The game clock shall be stopped: at the expiration of time for each period and when an official signals time-out. For a charged time-out, the timer shall start a time-out watch and shall direct the scores to signal the referee when it is time to resume play.

d. The timers shall indicate with a gong, pistol, or siren the expiration of playing time. If the timer's signal fails to sound, or not heard, the timer shall use other means to notify the referee immediately. If, in the meantime, a goal has been made or a foul has occurred, the referee shall consult the timer. If the timer agrees that time expired before the ball was in flight, the goal shall not count. If they agree that the period ended before the foul occurred, the foul shall be disregarded unless it was unsportsmanlike. If there is disagreement the goal shall count or the foul shall be penalized unless the referee has other knowledge.

NOTE: However, in a dead ball situation, if the clock shows :00 the period or game is considered to have ended although the buzzer may not have sounded.

e. Record only actual playing time in the last two minutes of the fourth period and the last two minutes of any overtime period or periods.

NOTE: Clock will be stopped immediately without signal from official, on all violations.

1. Federation	—Two referees are used with the third being optional.
NCAA	—Two referees are used with the third being optional.
NBA	—Three referees are used.

RULE NO. 3—PLAYERS, SUBSTITUTES AND COACHES

Section I—Team

Each team shall consist of five players, one of whom shall be designated as the captain. No team may be reduced to less than five players. If and when a player in the game receives his sixth personal foul and all substitutes have already been disqualified, said player remains in the game and is charged with a personal and team foul. A technical foul also is assessed against his team. All subsequent personal fouls shall be treated similarly. All players who have six or more personal fouls and remain in game shall be treated similarly.

In the event a player is injured and must leave the game, he must be replaced by the last player who was disqualified by reason of receiving six personal fouls. Each subsequent requirement to replace an injured player will be treated in this inverse order. Any such re-entry in a game by a disqualified player shall be penalized by a technical foul.

Section II—Starting Line-Ups

At least ten minutes before the game is scheduled to begin the scorers shall be supplied with the name and number of each player who may participate in the game. Starting line-ups will be indicated. Failure to comply with this provision should be reported to the Commissioner.

Section III—The Captain

a. Only the designated captain may talk to an official during a time out charged to his team.

b. He may discuss a rule interpretation but not a judgment play.

c. If the captain and the official are not in agreement, the coach may then enter an official protest and the game continues to completion. The official will then inform the official scorer and have it entered into the offical scorebook with time, score and rule quoted. The public address announcer will be instructed to inform the spectators that the game is being played under protest.

Section IV—The Coach and Others

a. A coach must remain in the immediate vicinity (area directly in front) of his bench at all times.

NOTE: A coach may go to the scorer's table only to check statistical items.

b. A coach is not permitted to talk to an official during any time-out. (See Sec. 3(a) for captain's rights).

c. A playing coach will have no special privileges. He is to conduct himself in the same manner as any other player.

d. Any club personnel not seated on the bench must conduct themselves so as not to reflect unfavorably on the dignity of the game or that of the officials. Violations by any of the personnel indicated shall require a written report to the Commissioner for subsequent action.

e. The bench shall be occupied only by the coach, assistant coach, players and trainer.

Section V — Substitutes

a. A substitute shall report to the scorer, giving his name, number and who he is to replace. The scorer shall sound the horn as soon as the ball is dead to indicate a substitution. The horn does not have to be sounded between quarters and halves. No substitute may enter a game after a field goal by either team, unless the ball is dead due to a technical foul. He may enter after the 1st of 2 or more free throws, whether made or missed.

b. The substitute shall remain outside the boundary lines until he is beckoned on by an official. If the ball is about to become alive, the beckoning signal shall be withheld.

NOTE: A substitute must be ready to enter when beckoned. He must have discarded any articles of clothing he will not wear on the playing floor. No delays for removal of sweat clothes will be permitted.

c. The substitute shall not replace a free throw shooter or a player involved in a jump ball.

d. Once the substitute has been beckoned onto court, he must enter the game and cannot be removed until the next dead ball.

NOTE: A subsitute **can be** recalled from the scorer's table prior to being beckoned in the game.

e. Any player who fails to properly report to the scorer as shown in (a) above shall be subject to a $25 fine on recommendation of the official scorer. Any player who doesn't wait until he is properly beckoned on the floor by the referee as in (b) above shall be charged with a technical foul.

NOTE: Notification of all above infractions and ensuing procedures shall be in accordance with Rule II, Section 7.

QUESTION: May a substituion be made during an official's time-out?

ANSWER: No.

Section VI — Jerseys

a. Each player shall be numbered on the front and back of his jersey with a number of solid color contrasting with the color of the shirt.

b. Each number must be not less than ¾" in width and not less than 6" in height on both front and back. Each player shall have his surname affixed to the back of his game jersey in letters at least 2" in height.

c. The home team shall wear light color jerseys with the visitors dressed in dark jerseys. For neutral court games and doubleheaders the 2nd team named in the official schedule shall be regarded as the home team and shall wear the light colored jerseys.

1. Federation	—Teams may play with less than 5 players if no substitutes are available.
NCAA	—Teams may play with less than 5 players if no substitutes are available.
NBA	—Teams must always have 5 players on the court.
2. Federation	—Uniform regulations as to style, colors, and numbers.
NCAA	—Uniform regulations as to style, colors, and numbers.
NBA	—No uniform regulations.

Rules

RULE NO. 4—DEFINITIONS

Section I—Basket

A team's own basket is the ring and net through which its players try to throw the ball. The visiting team has the choice of basket for the first half.

The teams change baskets for the second half.

NOTE: The basket selected by the visiting team when **first entering upon the court** shall be their basket for the first half.

Section II—Blocking

Blocking is personal contact which impedes the progress of an opponent.

Section III—Dribble

A dribble is ball movement caused by a player IN CONTROL who throws or taps the ball in the air or to the floor and then touches it once before the dribble ends. The dribble ends when the dribbler: (a) touches the ball with both hands simultaneously, or (b) permits it to come to rest while he is in contact with it, or (c) tries for goal, or (d) otherwise loses control, or when ball becomes dead.

QUESTION (1)—Is a player dribbling while tapping the ball during a jump, or when a pass rebounds from his hand or when he fumbles or when he taps a rebound or a pass away from other players who are attempting to get it?

ANSWER—No, the player is not in control under these conditions.

QUESTION (2)—Is it a dribble when a player stands still and: (a) bounces the ball; or (b) holds the ball and touches it to the floor once or more?

ANSWER—(a) Yes; (b) No.

QUESTION (3)—May a dribbler alternate hands?

ANSWER—Yes.

QUESTION (4)—May a player touch the ball more than once while dribbling before it touches the floor?

ANSWER—No.

Section IV—Fouls

a. A personal foul is a foul which involves contact with an opponent.

b. A technical foul is a foul which does not involve contact with an opponent and can be assessed against player and against non-player who is on the bench.

c. A double foul is a situation in which two opponents commit personal or technical fouls against each other at approximately the same time.

d. Offensive foul is a foul committed by a player while he or a teammate is in control of the ball.

Section V—Free Throw

A free throw is the privilege given a player to score one point by an unhindered throw for goal from a position directly behind the free throw line.

Section VI—Front/Back Court

a. A team's front court consists of that part of the court between its end line and the nearer edge of the center line, including its basket and inbounds part of the backboard. A team's back court consists of the entire division line and the rest of the court to include opponent's basket and inbounds part of backboard.

NOTE: A ball which is in contact with a player or with the court is in the back court if either the ball or the player is touching the back court. It is in the front court if neither the ball nor the player is touching the back court.

A ball which is not in contact with a player or the court retains the same status as when it was last in contact with a player or the court.

QUESTION—From the front court, a player passes the ball across the division line, it touches a teammate who is in the air after leaping from the back court or it touches an official in the back court. Is the ball in the back court?

ANSWER—Yes. The location of a player is determined by the point where his foot is touching the floor. When he is in the air from a leap, he retains the same status as when he last touched the floor as far as the boundary or the division line or the free throw line is connected. The location of an official is determined in the same manner as that of a player. Hence, if the official is touching the back court of the team in control, he is in the back court. When the ball touches an official it is the same as touching the floor at the official's location.

b. A team must bring the ball across the center line within 10 seconds. If, however, the defensive player causes the ball to go out of bounds in the back court, the offensive team will still be allowed 10 seconds to bring the ball across the center line.

Section VII—Held Ball

Held ball occurs when two opponents have one or both hands firmly on the ball.

NOTE: Held ball should not be called until both players have both hands so firmly on the ball that neither can gain sole possession without undue roughness. If a player is lying or sitting on the floor while in possession, he should have opportunity to throw the ball, but held ball should be called if there is danger of injury.

Section VIII—Pivot

A pivot takes place when a player who is holding the ball steps once or more than once in any direction with the same foot, the other foot, called the pivot foot, being kept at its point of contact with the floor.

Section IX—Traveling

Running with ball is progressing in any direction in excess of prescribed limits while holding the ball. The limits follow: (a.) A player who receives the ball while standing still may pivot, using either foot as the pivot foot. (b.) A player who receives the ball while he is progressing or upon completion of a dribble may use a two-count rhythm in coming to a stop or in getting rid of the ball. The first count occurs:

(1) As he receives the ball if either foot is touching the floor at the time he receives it;

(2) As the foot touches the floor or as both feet touch the floor simultaneously after he receives the ball if both feet are off the floor when he receives it.

The second count occurs when, after the count of one, either foot touches the floor or both feet touch the floor simultaneously.

When a player comes to a stop on the count of one he may pivot and may use either foot as the pivot foot.

When a player comes to a stop on the count of two, if one foot is in advance of the other he may pivot but the rear foot only may be used as the pivot foot; however, if neither foot is in advance of the other he may use either foot as the pivot foot.

c.(1) A player who receives the ball while standing still, or who comes to a legal stop while holding the ball, may lift the pivot foot or jump when he throws for goal or passes, but the ball must leave his hands before the pivot foot again touches the floor, or before either foot again touches the floor if the player has jumped;

(2) In starting a dribble after receiving the ball while standing still, or after coming to a legal stop, a player may not jump before the ball leaves his hands, nor may he lift the pivot from the floor before the ball leaves his hands.

(3) If a player does not pass or shoot when leaving floor with ball, he is guilty of traveling.

QUESTION (1)—Is it traveling if a player falls to the floor while holding the ball?

ANSWER—No. Unless he makes progress by sliding.

QUESTION (2)—A1 jumps to throw the ball. B1 prevents the throw by placing one or both hands firmly on the ball so that (a) A1; or (b) A1 and B1 both return to the floor holding it.

ANSWER—Held ball. However, if A1 voluntarily drops the ball before he returns to the floor and he then touches the ball before it is touched by another player, A1 has commited a traveling violation.

Section X—Screen

A screen is legal action of a player who, without causing undue contact, delays or prevents an opponent from reaching a desired position.

Section XI—Try for Goal

A try for field goal is a player's attempt to throw the ball into his basket for a field goal. The try starts when the player begins the motion which habitually precedes the actual throw. It continues until the throwing effort ceases. The term is also used to include the movement of the ball in flight until it has become dead or has been touched by a player.

Section XII—Throw-In

A throw-in is a method of putting ball in play from out of bounds in accordance with Rule No. 6. The throw-in begins when the ball is at the disposal of the team or player entitled to it and ends when the passed ball touches or is touched by an inbounds player other than the thrower in.

No major rule differences.

RULE NO. 5—SCORING AND TIMING

Section I—Scoring

a. A legal goal is made when a live ball enters the basket from above and remains in or passes through.

b. A goal from the field counts two points for the team into whose basket the ball is thrown.

c. A goal from the free throw line counts one point for the thrower's team.

Rules

NOTE: If a free throw attempt is unsuccessful and while the ball is in the air it is tapped into the basket by a player who has not obtained complete control of the ball with both feet touching the floor, the basket, if scored, shall count two points and shall be credited to the player tapping the ball in.

QUESTION—A player makes a free throw in his opponent's basket. Does the point count for his opponent?

ANSWER—No. If the mistake is discovered before time is in, the error should be corrected and player required to make attempt at his own basket.

NOTE: Goals from the field, thrown in an opponent's basket shall be credited to the opponent's score and mentioned in a footnote. Basket is credited to opponent nearest the shooter. Any field goal that, in the opinion of the officials, is intentionally scored in the wrong basket shall be disallowed.

NOTE: If a discrepancy in the score cannot be resolved, the running score shall be official.

Section II — Timing

a. All quarters of regulation play in the NBA will be twelve minutes.

b. All overtime periods of play will be five minutes.

c. Fifteen minutes will be permitted between halves of all games.

d. Ninety seconds will be permitted between all quarters and for time-outs.

EXCEPTION: Injury (20 seconds), disqualification (30 seconds).

NOTE: In the case of a split-second situation, the 47th minute of a game does not start until after the second hand has actually progressed beyond the 60 second mark of the 46th minute.

NOTE: The public address operator is required to announce the fact that there are two minutes remaining in regulation or overtime periods.

Section III — End of Period

a. Each period ends when time expires.

EXCEPTIONS:

(1) If a live ball is in flight, the period ends when the goal is made or missed.

(2) If a foul occurs at approximately the instant time expires for a period, the period officially ends after the free throw or throws are attempted.

NOTE: No line-up of players will be permitted in conditions outlined in (2) above.

(3) If the ball is in the air when the buzzer sounds ending a period and it subsequently is touched by a defensive player, the goal, if successful, shall count.

(4) If a time-out request is made at approximately the instant time expires for a period, the period ends and the time-out shall not be granted.

NOTE: When the ball is dead and the game clock shows :00, the period has ended even though the buzzer may not have sounded.

Section IV — Tie Score

If the score is tied at the end of the 4th quarter, play shall resume in 90 seconds without change of baskets for one or more periods whichever is needed to determine a winner. (See Rule 5, Sec II (d) for amount of time between overtime quarters.)

Rules

QUESTION—With the score tied, a foul is committed near the expiration of time in the fourth quarter. If free throw is successful, should an extra period be played?

ANSWER—If the foul occurs before the ball becomes dead and the fourth quarter is ended, no extra period is played. However, if the foul occurs after the fourth quarter has ended, the extra period must be played whether the foul shot is made or not.

Section V—Time-Out

a. Time-out occurs and the timing instruments shall be stopped when:

(1) A foul is called.

(2) A jump ball is called.

(3) Granting of a player's request for a time-out, such request being granted only when the ball is dead or in control of the requesting player's team. The scoring team cannot stop play immediately after scoring, by calling a time-out or making a substitution. The team scored upon shall have the opportunity to put the ball in play.

(4) An unusual delay in getting the ball into play after a field goal.

(5) On all floor violations (whenever official's whistle sounds, goal tending included).

(6) Time-out for injury or any other emergency. (Official's time.)

NOTE: When a defensive player is injured, the officials shall not stop play **under any circumstances** until after a goal is scored or the ball becomes dead.

NOTE: If on a jump ball or foul shot situation a player is injured and must be removed from the game, the opposing coach selects his replacement. The injured player cannot return to the game. Exception: If the player is injured due to a flagrant foul he may reenter the game at any time.

(7) During the last two minutes of the regulation game or any overtime period, a field goal is scored.

NOTE: Whenever a team is granted a time-out, play shall not resume until the full 90 seconds have elapsed.

(8) No time-out will be charged if it is called to correct a wrong interpretation of a call and correction is sustained.

(9) A coach shall have 30 seconds to replace a disqualified player.

b. Time-out shall not be granted:

(1) After a score of any kind to the team that has scored.

(2) Unless the team has possession of the ball.

(3) When a player of the team not in possession is injured, until a goal is scored or the ball becomes dead or his team gains possession.

NOTE: If a request for time-out is made it should be ignored. However, if an official upon receiving a time-out request, inadvertently blows his whistle, play shall be suspended and the team in possession shall put the ball into play immediately at the sideline nearest where the ball was when the time-out was called. The team in possession shall have only the time remaining of the original ten seconds in which to move the ball to front court. The 24 second clock shall remain the same.

Section VI—Time-Out Charged

a. A team shall be charged with a time-out for each request approved.

b. When a player is injured, he must resume play or be replaced by a substitute within 20 seconds or an automatic time-out will be charged to his team. The 20-second injury time-out is limited to one per team per half: if the injured player is taken out of the game the opposing team may also substitute one player at that interval. Both teams can use this time-out only charged to team calling it.

c. Following a time-out call for injury, a team may only substitute for the injured player. If substitution is made, opponent may also substitute.

d. Only one injured player from the same team may be replaced during a 20-second injury time-out. If two players on the same team are injured at the same time and the coach wishes to replace both, he must do it via a charged time-out.

e. If a second injury time-out is called during a half, it automatically becomes a charged time-out. Overtimes are considered extensions of the second half.

f. The referee shall instruct the timer to record the 20 seconds and to inform him when the time has expired.

g. This rule also includes searching for lost contact lens.

NOTE: No time-out will be permitted to allow any player to adjust his clothing or equipment (shoes, laces, glasses, etc.).

Section VII—Time-In

a. After time has been out, the game clock shall be started when the official signals time-in; the timer is authorized to start game clock if officials neglect to signal.

b. On a free throw that is unsuccessful and the ball is to continue in play, the clock shall be started when the missed free throw is touched by any player.

c. If play is resumed by a throw-in from out of bounds, the clock shall be started when the ball touches a player within the playing area of the court.

d. Time-out during the last two minutes of regulation play or overtimes (see 5, VIII-d.). The last two minutes begin when the clock shows 2:00 minutes to play.

Section VIII—Authorized Time-Outs

a. Each team may be granted seven (7) charged time-outs during regulation play. Each team is limited to no more than four (4) time-outs in the fourth quarter and no more than three (3) time-outs in the last two minutes of regulation play.

b. In overtime periods each team shall be allowed two (2) time-outs regardless of the number of time-outs called or remaining during the regulation play or previous overtimes. There is no restriction as to when a team must call its time-outs during any overtime period.

NOTE: Additional time-outs may be granted at the expense of a technical foul and all privileges apply. (Exception: see Rule 12A, II)

c. Each team must take at least one time-out per quarter. If neither team has taken a time-out during the first five minutes of each of the four regulation quarters, it shall be mandatory for the official scorer to take a time-out before the sixth minute of play is completed. Time-out is charged to the home team. If neither team has taken a second time-out before the ninth minute of play, it shall be mandatory for the official scorer to take a time-out before the tenth minute of play has elapsed. Time-out is charged to the visiting team. If one team takes two time-outs during any single period, it is not mandatory for the official scorer to take a time-out.

d. Time-out in back court: during the last two minutes of regulation play or overtimes, if a team requests a time-out after the ball is out-of-bounds or IMMEDIATELY after getting the ball from a rebound or change of possession, time-out shall be granted, and upon resumption of play, they shall have the option of putting the ball into play at midcourt or at the out of bounds spot.

However, once the ball is thrown in from out-of-bounds or the ball is advanced after receiving it from a rebound or change of possession and a time-out request is granted—upon resumption of play, the ball shall be put into play at the spot nearest where the ball was when time-out was called, and the time shall remain as it was when the time-out was called.

QUESTION—During the last two minutes of regulation play, team A attempts a field goal. The ball rebounds to the corner of team B's backcourt where B secures possession and immediately requests a timeout. Where is the ball put into play?

ANSWER—The team calling the time-out, upon resumption of play, shall have the **option** of putting the ball into play on that side of the court where the ball was when time-out was called or moving the ball to midcourt on that side of the court. However, if the time-out request was made immediately after a score, the team scored upon would have the **option** of putting the ball into play at the division line on either side of the court or at the endline.

NOTE: In both situations, time-out is granted.

QUESTION—A player receives the ball from a throw-in in the backcourt or from a rebound or change of possession and a time-out request is granted, where is the ball put into play after the resumption of time?

ANSWER—Ball is put into play, after the time-out, at the spot nearest where the ball was when time-out was called.

In the case where possession may change, with the ball still in play, the team now in possession may call a time-out without penalty.

If a legal time-out is called in the backcourt in the last two minutes of regulation play or over-times, the team shall have the option of moving the ball to mid-court. At all other times, the ball shall be passed in from a point out-of-bounds nearest to where the ball was when the time-out was called.

NOTE: (1) The official scorer shall notify a team when it has been charged with a time-out.

(2) A time-out shall not be called by the official scorer after a score of any kind, except after a free throw that is to be followed by another free throw attempt.

(3) When the clock shows 2:00 remaining in regulation play or overtimes, we are in the 2:00 minute period.

---

1. Federation—Eight minute quarters with three minute overtimes are used.
   NCAA —Twenty minute halves with five minute overtimes are used.
   NBA —Twelve minute quarters with five minute overtimes are used.
2. Federation—Rule covering lack of sufficient action to prevent stalling.
   NCAA —Rule covering lack of sufficient action to prevent stalling.
   NBA —No rule covering lack of sufficient action.

RULE NO. 6—PUTTING BALL IN PLAY—LIVE/DEAD BALL

Section I—Start of Games/Quarters and Others

a. The game and overtimes shall be started with a jump ball in the center circle.

b. The team which gains possession after the opening tap will put the ball into play at their opponent's end line to begin the fourth quarter. The team losing the opening tap will put the ball into play at their opponent's end line at the beginning of the second and third quarters.

Rules

NOTE: In putting the ball into play, the thrower-in may run along the end line or pass it to a teammate who is also out-of-bounds at the end line, — as after a score.

c. After any dead ball, play shall be resumed by a jump, a throw-in or by placing ball at the disposal of a free-thrower.

d. On any violation except where the ball goes out-of-bounds at the endline or defensive goal-tending is called, the ball shall be put into play at the sideline.

Section II — Live Ball

a. The ball becomes alive when:

(1) Tossed by an official on any jump ball.

NOTE: Clock starts only when tapped. (See Rule 5)

(2) Ball is placed at the disposal of designated player for throw-in.

(3) Ball is placed at the disposal of a free-throw shooter.

Section III — Jump Balls in Center Circle

a. The ball shall be put in play in the center circle by a jump between two opponents:

(1) at the start of the game.

(2) at the start of each overtime period.

Section IV — Other Jump Balls

a. The ball shall be put in play by a jump ball at the circle which is closest to the spot where:

(1) a held ball occurs.

(2) a ball out of bounds caused by both teams.

(3) after a double foul situation on the ball, by both involved players.

(4) a double free-throw violation occurs.

(5) the ball lodges in a basket support.

(6) the ball becomes dead when neither team is in control and no goal or infraction is involved.

(7) unless both officials have conflicting possession decisions.

NOTE: In (1) or (2) the jump ball shall be between the two involved players unless injury precludes one of the jumpers from participation. If injured player must leave the game, the coach of the opposing team shall select from his opponent's bench a player who will replace the injured player. The injured player will not be permitted to re-enter the game.

Section V — Restrictions Governing Jump Balls

a. Each jumper must have one, but may have both feet on or inside that half of the jumping circle which is farthest from his own basket.

b. The ball must be tapped by one or both of the players participating in jump ball after it reaches its highest point. If ball falls to floor without being tapped by at least one of the jumpers, the official off the ball shall whistle the ball dead and signal another toss.

c. Neither jumper may tap the tossed ball before it reaches its highest point.

d. Neither jumper may leave the circle until the ball has been tapped.

e. Neither jumper may catch the tossed ball nor tapped ball until such time as it has been touched by one of the eight non-jumpers, the floor, the basket or the backboard.

f. Neither jumper is permitted to tap ball more than twice on any jump ball.

g. The eight non-jumpers will remain outside the restraining circle until the ball has been tapped. Teammates may not occupy adjacent positions around the restraining circle if an opponent desires one of the positions.

Penalty for c., d., e., f., g.: Ball awarded out of bounds to opponent.

QUESTION—During a jump ball is a jumper required to (a) face his own basket; (b) jump and attempt to tap ball?

ANSWER—(a) No specific facing is required, (b) No. But if neither jumper taps the ball, it must be tossed again with both jumpers being ordered to jump.

NOTE: During any jump ball situation officials shall sound whistle only if an infraction that occurs benefits offending team.

Section VI—Dead Ball

a. The ball becomes dead or remains dead when:

(1) held ball occurs or ball lodges between the basket and backboard.

(2) time expires for a quarter, half or extra period.

(3) there is an unsuccessful attempt: (a) on a free throw for technical foul or (b) a free throw which is to be followed by another throw.

(4) a foul occurs.

(5) a floor violation (traveling, 3 secs, 24 secs, 10 secs, etc.) occurs or there is basket interference or a free throw violation by the thrower's team.

(6) Any goal is made in the last two minutes of the fourth quarter.

EXCEPTION: The ball does not become dead when (2), occurs after a live ball is in flight.

QUESTION—If the ball is in flight and on its downward path on a field goal try by Team A and the period expires, does the goal count if the ball is touched by: Team A or Team B?

ANSWER—It is basket interference when touched by Team B. No points scored if touched by Team A.

> No major rule differences.

RULE NO. 7—24 SECOND CLOCK

Section I—Definition

For the purpose of clarification the 24-second device shall be referred to as "the 24 second clock."

Section II—Starting and Stopping of 24 Second Clock

a. The 24 second clock will start when a team gains possession of the ball.

b. A team in possession of the ball must attempt a shot to score within 24 seconds after gaining possession of the ball. To constitute a legal shot to score, the following conditions must be complied with:

(1) The ball must leave the player's hand prior to the expiration of 24 seconds.

(2) After leaving the player's hand the ball must hit the rim or a legal surface of the backboard. If it does not and the 24 seconds expires there has been a violation committed.

c. A team is considered in possession of the ball when holding, passing or dribbling.

NOTE: In the case of passing or dribbling, the team is considered in possession of the ball even though the ball has been batted away but the opponent has not gained possession. No three second violation can occur under these conditions.

d. Team control ends when:

(1) there is a try for field goal.

(2) opponent gains possession.

(3) ball becomes dead.

e. If a ball is touched by a defensive player who does not gain possession of the ball, the 24 second clock shall continue to run.

f. If a defensive player causes the ball to go out of bounds, the 24 second clock is stopped and the offensive team shall, on regaining the ball for throw-in, have the unexpired time or 5 seconds, whichever is longer, to attempt a shot.

g. If during any quarter there are 24 seconds OR LESS left to play in the quarter, the 24 second clock shall not function.

NOTE: If an official inadvertently blows his whistle and the 24-second clock buzzer sounds while the ball is in air, play shall be suspended and play resumed by a jump ball between any two opponents in the nearest free throw circle if shot is unsuccessful. If the shot is successful, the goal shall count and the whistle is ignored. It should be noted that even though the official blows his whistle, all provisions of the above rule apply.

h. If there is a question whether or not an attempt to score has been made within the 24 seconds allowed the final decision shall be made by the referee.

i. On a throw-in, the 24 second clock shall start when the ball touches a player on the court.

j. Any time a personal foul is called the clock is to be re-set to 24 seconds.

k. Any time a technical foul is called the clock shall remain as is or be reset to 10 seconds, whichever is greater.

l. Whenever the 24 second clock shows 0, the 24-second time has expired even though the horn may not have sounded.

Section III—Putting Ball In Play After Violation

If a team fails to attempt a shot within the time allotted, the ball shall be taken out of bounds on the side of the court nearest to the spot where the play was suspended and handed to the thrower-in.

Section IV—Resetting 24 Second Clock

An official shall have the power to reset the 24 second clock to cover any special situation that he thinks warrants such action. On all technical fouls the 24 second clock shall remain the same as when play was stopped or re-set to 10 seconds, whichever is greater. The 24-second clock shall be re-set to 24 seconds on all violations, as well as after a zone warning.

1. Federation—No rule.	
NCAA	—No rule.
NBA	—A team in possession must try for a goal within 24 seconds of obtaining control of the ball.

Rules

RULE NO. 8—OUT-OF-BOUNDS AND THROW-IN

Section I—Player

a. The player is out of bounds when he touches the floor or any object on or outside a boundary. For location of a player in the air his position is that from which he last touched the floor.

Section II—Ball

a. The ball is out of bounds when it touches a player who is out of bounds or any other person, the floor, or any object on, above or outside of a boundary or the supports or back of the backboard.

NOTE: Any ball that rebounds or passes behind or over the backboard from any point is considered out of bounds.

QUESTION—Ball glances off face of the backboard and across boundary line, but before it touches the floor or any obstruction out of bounds it is caught by a player who is inbounds. Is the ball inbounds or out of bounds?

ANSWER—Inbounds.

b. The ball is caused to go out of bounds by the last player to touch it before it goes out, provided it is out of bounds because of touching something other than a player. If the ball is out of bounds because of touching a player who is on or outside a boundary, such player caused it to go out.

c. If the ball goes out of bounds and was last touched simultaneously by two opponents, both of whom are inbounds or out of bounds, or if the official is in doubt as to who last touched the ball, or if the officials disagree, play shall be resumed by a jump ball between the two involved players in the nearest restraining circle.

d. After the ball is out of bounds the official shall designate a **nearby opponent of the player who committed the violation** and he shall make the throw-in at the spot out of bounds nearest where the ball crossed the boundary.

e. After any playing court violation, the ball is to be put into play at the sideline.

Section III—The Throw-In

a. The throw-in starts when the ball is at the disposal of a player entitled to the throw-in. He shall pass it inbounds within 5 seconds from the time the throw-in starts. Until the passed ball has crossed the plane of the boundary no player shall have any part of his person over the boundary line and the teammates shall not occupy adjacent positions near the boundary if an opponent desires one of the positions.

b. On out of bound plays the ball shall be put in play at the point where the ball crossed a boundary line and not from original throw-in spot.

c. After a score, field goal or free throw, the latter coming as the result of a personal foul, any player of the team not credited with the score shall put the ball into play from any point out of bounds at the end line of the court where the goal was made. He may pass the ball to a teammate behind the end line, however, the 5 second pass-in rule applies.

d. After a free throw violation by the throwing team, the throw-in is made from out of bounds at either end of the free throw line extended.

e. Any ball out of bounds in a team's front court cannot be passed into the back court. On all back-court rule violations, the ball shall be given to opposing team at center court and must be passed into the front court.

NOTE: Penalty for violating this rule is loss of ball to opposing team a point of infraction.

> No major rule differences.

RULE NO. 9—FREE THROW

Section I—Positions

When a free throw is awarded, an official shall take the ball to the free throw line of the offended team. After allowing reasonable time for the players to take their positions, he shall put the ball in play by placing it at the disposal of the free throw shooter. The same procedure shall be followed for each free throw of a multiple throw. During a free throw for personal foul, each of the spaces perpendicular to the end line must be occupied by an opponent of the free thrower. Teammates of the free thrower must occupy the next adjacent spaces on each side. It is not mandatory for the defensive team to occupy the third adjacent space. However, no teammates of the free thrower are permitted in these spaces. No more than three defensive team players are allowed on the free throw lanes. All other players not stationed on the free throw lanes must be at least six feet from the foul shooter and/or the free throw lanes or foul circle.

NOTE: If the ball is to become dead after the last free throw, players shall not take positions along the free-throw lane.

EXAMPLE: Technical fouls and for fouls called at end of quarters where clock runs out and no time remains.

Section II—Shooting of Free Throw

a. The free throw or throws awarded because of a personal foul shall be attempted by the offended player. If such player must withdraw because of disqualification, he must attempt the throw(s) before retiring from the game.

NOTE: If a player is fouled and injured on the same play and cannot shoot the awarded shots, the opposing coach shall select from his opponent's bench the player who will replace the injured player and this player will attempt the shot(s). The injured player will not be permitted to re-enter the game, unless such injury is a result of a flagrant act of an opponent.

b. A foul try, personal or technical, shall neither be legal nor count unless an official handles the ball and is also in the free throw area when foul try is attempted.

c. When a player is allowed three attempts to make two points, if the shooter or a member of his team causes a violation to occur on one of the two attempts, and a foul goal is nullified, the third shot must be taken.

Section III—Time Limit

The try for goal shall be made within 10 seconds after the ball has been placed at the disposal of the free thrower at the free throw line; this applies to each free throw.

Section IV—Next Play

After a free throw which is not followed by another free throw, the ball shall be put in play by a throw-in: as after a field goal if the try is successful.

EXCEPTION: After a free throw for a foul which occurs during a dead ball which immediately precedes any period, the ball shall be put into play by the team entitled to the throw-in in the period which follows. (See Rule 6, Section I (b)).

> No major rule differences.

RULE NO. 10—VIOLATIONS AND PENALTIES

Section I—A Player Shall Not:

A. Violate the free throw provisions:

    (1) After the ball is placed at the disposal of a free thrower, he shall throw within 10 seconds in such a way that the ball enters the basket or touches the ring before it is touched by a player.

    (2) Touch the ball or basket while the ball is on or within the basket.

    (3) Touch the floor on or across the free throw line or lanes.

NOTE: The restriction in (3) above applies until the ball leaves the free thrower's hands, except for the free thrower who may not cross the free throw line until the ball touches the ring or backboard or the free throw ends.

    (4) Disconcert the free thrower in any way once the ball has been placed at the disposal of the free-thrower shooter.

PENALTY:

a. In (1), (2), (3), (4) if violation by offense, no point can be scored. Ball is awarded out of bounds to opponents opposite free throw line extended.

b. In (1), (2), (3), (4), if violation is by defense and throw is successful, disregard violation; if throw is unsuccessful, substitute throw shall be attempted.

NOTE:

a. If there is a violation by each team, ball becomes dead, no point can be scored, play shall be resumed by a jump ball between any two opponents in nearest free throw circle.

b. The out of bounds in "a" under Penalty and the jump ball provision in "a" above do not apply if the free throw is to be followed by another free throw or if there are free throws by both teams.

B. Cause the ball to go out of bounds.

QUESTION—Dribbler in control steps on or outside a boundary, but does not touch the ball while he is out of bounds, returns in-bounds and continues dribbling. Is this a violation?

ANSWER—Yes.

C. Violate provisions of putting ball in play from out of bounds.

    (1) Thrower-in shall not carry ball into the court nor fail to pass it within 5 seconds, nor touch it in the court before it has touched another player.

    (2) No player shall have any part of his person over the boundary line before the ball has been passed across the line.

    (3) After an official has designated a player to throw ball in, there shall be no change of player unless a time-out by either team has subsequently been called.

    (4) A player shall not step or run over any boundary line while putting ball in play.

PENALTY: Loss of ball (The ball is put into play at the point of infraction).

D. Run with ball, kick it, or strike it with the fist.

NOTE: Kicking the ball or blocking it with any part of a player's leg is a violation when it is a positive act; accidentally striking the ball with the foot or leg is not a violation.

E. Dribble a second time after his first dribble has ended, unless it is after he has lost control: (a) through a try for field goal at his own basket; or (b) through a bat by an opponent; or (c) through a pass or fumble which has then touched another player.

F. Violate provisions governing jump ball situations:

(1) If both teams violate the jumping rule, or if the official makes a bad toss, the toss should be repeated;

(2) If a foul is committed on any jump ball, it shall result in the loss of the ball for the offending team and the offended team shall be awarded the ball at the sideline nearest the jumping circle.

NOTE: To be treated as a loose ball foul.

G. Remain for more than 3 seconds in that part of his free throw lane between the end line and the farther edge of the free throw line while the ball is in control of his team.

NOTE: Allowance may be made for a player who, having been in the restricted area for less than 3 seconds is in the act of shooting at the end of the third second.

NOTE: Three second count shall not begin until the ball is in control in the offensive team's front court.

QUESTION—Does the 3-second restriction apply: (a) to a player who has only one foot touching the lane boundary; or (b) while the ball is dead or is in flight on a try or while the ball is loose?

ANSWER—(a) Yes, the line is part of the lane. (b) No, the team is not in control.

H. Be in continuous control of a ball which is in his back court for more than 10 consecutive seconds.

I. Be the first to touch a ball which he or a teammate caused to go from front court to back court while his team was in control of the ball.

EXCEPTION: This restriction does not apply if, after a jump ball in the center circle, the player who first secures control of the tapped ball is in his front court at the time he secures such control and causes the ball to go to his back court, not later than the first loss of control by him and provided it is the first time the ball is in his back court following the jump ball. Once said player establishes a positive offensive position this exception does not apply.

NOTE: During a jump ball, a try for goal or a situation in which a player taps the ball away from congested area, as during rebounding, in an attempt to get the ball out where player control may be secured, the ball is not in control of either team. Hence the restriction on first touching does not apply.

QUESTION—Player A receives pass in his front court and throws ball to his back court where ball: (a) is touched by a teammate; or (b) goes directly out of bounds; or (c) lies or bounces with all players hesitating to touch it.

ANSWER—Violation when touched in (a). In (b) it is a violation for going out of bounds. In (c) ball is alive so that B may secure control. If A touches ball first, it is a violation. In either case, 24 second clock continues to run and rules apply.

PENALTY: Items D. thru G. Ball becomes dead when violation occurs. Ball is awarded to opponent at out of bounds spot nearest violation.

J. Use "STICK-UM" or any similar substance.

PENALTY: Fine of $25 for first violation, doubled for each subsequent violation upon notification to Commissioner by either official.

K. Excessive and/or vigorous swinging of the elbows, without contact, is a violation.

L. If the ball enters the basket from below, a violation has occurred.

No major rule differences.

Rules

RULE NO. 11—BASKETBALL INTERFERENCE—GOAL TENDING

Section I—A Player Shall Not:

a. Touch the ball or basket when the ball is on or within either basket.

b. Touch the ball when it is touching the cylinder having the ring as its lower base.

EXCEPTION: In a or b if a player near his own basket has his hand legally in contact with the ball, it is not a violation if his contact with the ball continues after the ball enters the cylinder, or if, in such action, he touches the basket.

NOTE: Impetus factor by offensive player!

c. Touch the ball when it is not touching the cylinder but is in downward flight during a try for field goal while the entire ball is above the basket ring level and before the ball has touched the ring or the try has ended.

NOTE: For goal-tending to occur, the ball, in the judgment of the official, must have a chance to score. This section is not intended to conflict with paragraph (d) or (e) of Rule 11, Section I.

d. During a field goal attempt, touch a ball after it has touched any part of a backboard above ring level whether ball is considered on its upward or downward flight.

e. During a field goal attempt, touch a ball after it has touched the backboard below ring level and while ball is on its upward flight.

f. Trap ball against face of backboard.

NOTE: (1) To be a trapped ball three elements must exist simultaneously. The hand, the ball and the backboard must all occur at the same time. A batted ball against the backboard is not a trapped ball.

NOTE: (2) Any live ball from within the playing area that is in flight is considered to be a "field goal attempt" or trying for a goal.

PENALTY FOR ABOVE: If violation is at the opponent's basket, offended team is awarded two points. The crediting of the score and subsequent procedure is the same as if the awarded score has resulted from the ball having gone through the basket except that the official shall hand the ball to a player of the team entitled to the throw-in. If violation is at a team's own basket, no points can be scored and the ball is awarded to the offended team at the out of bounds spot on the side at either end of the free throw line extended. If there is a violation by both teams, play shall be resumed by a jump ball between any two opponents in the nearest circle.

No major rule differences.

RULE NO. 12—FOULS AND PENALTIES

A. Technical Foul

Section I—Zone Defenses

a. A zone defense is not permitted in NBA games. If an official is of the opinion that a team is guilty of violating this rule, he shall impose a technical foul on the team and, for the second violation, two technical fouls shall be imposed. Any recurrence of this violation will be penalized by two technical fouls and action by the Commissioner.

NOTE: Three basic principles govern the use of defensive alignments permitted in NBA games:

1. Any type of pressing defense is legal, whether it is a frontcourt press or backcourt press, and by any number of defensive players.

Rules

2. After the offensive team has advanced the ball into its frontcourt, a defensive player may not station himself in the 16-foot key area, longer than three seconds, if he is making no effort to play an opponent. The three-second count starts when the offensive team is in clear control of the ball in its frontcourt. Penalty: technical foul, and for every recurrence of the violation, two technical fouls shall be imposed.

3. When a ball has passed center court, no defensive player can guard an area of the court instead of guarding an opponent. Penalty: technical foul, and for every recurrence of the infraction, two technical fouls shall be imposed.

NOTE: The first two technicals are charged to the bench. On the third such infraction, coach is ejected.

Section II — Excessive Time-Outs

a. Requests for time out in excess of authorized number shall be granted. However, a technical foul penalty shall be assessed. A team is entitled to all regular time out privileges.

EXCEPTION: During the last two minutes of play and/or overtimes, if a team calls an excessive time out, the ball shall remain at the out-of-bounds spot where the ball was when the excessive time out was called.

Section III — Delay of Game

a. A player shall not delay the game by preventing ball from being promptly put into play such as:

(1) attempt to gain an advantage by interfering with ball after a goal.

(2) failing to immediately pass ball to the nearest official when a violation is called.

(3) bat ball away from an opponent before the player has the opportunity to in-bounds the ball.

Section IV — Substitutions

a. A substitute shall not enter the court without reporting to the scorer and being beckoned by an official.

b. A substitute shall not enter after having been disqualified.

c. It is the responsibility of each team to have the proper number of players on the court at all times.

NOTE: Penalty for failure to report to the scorer is $25 fine. No technical foul.

Section V — Basket Ring

a. Any player, who in the opinion of the officials, has deliberately hung on the basket ring shall be assessed a technical foul and a $100 fine.

Section VI — Conduct

A referee may assess a technical foul without prior warning at any time.

a. Officials may penalize, without prior warning, any act of unsportsmanlike conduct by anyone seated on the bench which, in the opinion of the officials, is detrimental to the game.

b. The first infraction shall be penalized by a technical foul and a $75 fine. The second infraction shall be penalized by a technical foul with violator expelled from the game and an additional $150 fine.

Rules

NOTE: (1) Technical foul called for: delay of game, or illegal defensive alignments are not considered acts of unsportsmanlike conduct in this case.

NOTE: (2) Two technicals for illegal defensive alignments (after one warning) result in ejection of the coach from the game.

    c. A technical foul shall be assessed for unsportsmanlike tactics such as:

        (1) disrespectfully addressing an official.

        (2) physically contacting an official.

        (3) overt actions indicating resentment to a call.

        (4) use of profanity.

        (5) a coach entering onto the court without permission of an official.

NOTE: (1) Cursing or blaspheming an official shall not be considered the only cause for imposing technical fouls. Running tirade, continuous criticism or griping may be sufficient cause to assess a technical. Flagrant misconduct shall result in ejection from the game.

NOTE: (2) Assessment of technical foul shall be avoided whenever and wherever possible, but when necessary they are to be applied without delay or procrastination.

NOTE: (3) If a personal foul and a technical foul are called aginst the same team at the same time, the technical foul shall be attempted first.

NOTE: (4) On technical foul attempts, whether the attempt has been successful or not, the ball shall be returned to the team having possession at the time the foul was called and play shall be resumed from a point out of bounds where play ended.

NOTE: (5) A foul which occurs when the ball is dead is a technical foul and must be unsportsmanlike in order to be penalized. Exception: fighting foul.

NOTE: (6) The shooter of a technical must be in the game when the technical is called.

NOTE: (7) A referee may eject a player or coach with only one technical.

QUESTION—May a player or a coach be ejected without the assessment of a technical foul?

ANSWER—No, ejection calls for the assessment of a technical foul.

Section VII—Fines

    a. Technical foul for unsportsmanlike conduct, violators are assessed a $75 fine for the first offense, and an additional $150 for the second offense in any one given game, for a total of $225 in fines. For ejection after the first technical foul, violators are assessed a $150 fine for a total of $225 in fines.

NOTE: Whether or not said player(s) are ejected, a fine not exceeding $10,000 and/or suspension may be imposed upon such player(s) by the Commissioner at his sole discretion.

    b. During a fight all players not involved must remain in vicinity of their bench. Violators will be assessed a $150 fine.

    c. A player, coach or assistant coach, upon being notified by an official that he has been ejected from the game, must leave the playing area IMMEDIATELY and remain in the dressing room of his team during such suspension until completion of the game. A fine not to exceed $10,000 and possible forfeiture of the game will be imposed for any violation of this rule.

    d. Any player who in the opinion of the officials has deliberately hung on the basket shall be assessed a technical foul and a fine of $100.

    e. Penalty for the use of "stickum" is a fine of $25 for the first violation, doubled for each subsequent violation.

f. Any player who fails to properly report to the scorer (Rule 3, V a.) shall be subject to a $25 fine on recommendation of the official scorer.

g. At half-time and the end of the game, the coach and his players are to leave the court and go directly to their dressing room without pause or delay. There is to be absolutely no talking to game officials.

PENALTY—$100 fine to be doubled for any additional violation.

h. Each player, when introduced prior to the start of the game,must be uniformly dressed.

PENALTY—$100 fine.

i. A $25 fine shall be assessed to any player(s) hanging on the rim during pre-game warm-up. One official shall be present during warm-up to observe. During the playoffs, the alternate official shall be assigned to this duty.

B. Personal Foul

Section I—Types

a. A player shall not hold, push, charge into, impede the progress of an opponent by extended arm, knee or by bending the body into a position that is not normal.

b. Contact caused by a defensive player approaching the ball holder from the rear is a form of pushing or holding.

c. Excessive use of elbows (2 shots if contact is made by elbows).

NOTE: A defensive player is permitted to retain contact with his opponent so long as he does not impede his opponent's progress. However, hand checking will be eliminated by rigid enforcement of this rule by all three officials. The illegal use of hands will not be permitted.

Section II—By Dribbler

A dribbler shall not charge into nor contact an opponent in his path nor attempt to dribble between two opponents or between an opponent and a boundary, unless the space is such as to provide a reasonable chance for him to go through without contact. If a dribbler, without contact, passes an opponent sufficiently to have head and shoulders in advance of him, the greater responsibility for subsequent contact is on the opponent. If a dribbler in his progress has established a straight line path, he may not be crowded out of that path but, if an opponent is able legally to establish a defensive position in that path, the dribbler must avoid contact by changing direction or ending his dribble.

Section III—By Screening

a. A player who screens shall not: (1) when he is behind a stationary opponent, take a position closer than a normal step from him; (2) when he assumes a position at the side or in front of a stationary opponent, make contact with him; (3) take a position so close to a moving opponent that this opponent cannot avoid contact by stopping or changing direction. In (3) the speed of the player to be screened will determine where the screener may take his stationary position. This position will vary and may be one to two normal steps or strides from his opponent. **(4) Move after assuming his screening position, except in the same direction and path of his opponent.**

b. If the screener violates any of these provisions and contact results, he has committed a personal foul.

1. Penalties for Sections 1-3

Offender is charged with one foul and if it is his sixth personal foul he is disqualified. Offended player is awarded one free throw providing it is not an offensive foul. A second free throw shall be awarded if the foul is:

a. Flagrant (fouls are to be attended whether the ball is dead,in possession or loose).

b. Against a field goal shooter whose attempt was not successful.

c. Swinging of elbows (contact must be made. Fouls are to be attempted whether the ball is dead, in possession or loose).

d. Back court (if team is in control of the ball in its back court and a foul is committed against a member of the team, it is a two shot foul Once the ball passes over the mid-court line from back-court to front-court, it shall then be considered to be **front-court control).**

e. Committed by a player whose team has exceeded the limit for team fouls per quarter. (See 2 below.)

f. Committed by a defensive player before ball is thrown in from out of bounds.

g. Against any offensive player who has a clear path to the basket thereby being deprived of the opportunity of scoring.

h. Undercutting an opponent.

NOTE: (1) If a player, coach or assistant coach, is ejected from a game or games, he shall not at any time before, during or after such game or games appear in any part of the auditorium or stands where his team is playing, during such ejection. A player, coach or assistant coach may only remain in the dressing room of his team during such suspension.

A violation of this rule shall call for an automatic fine of $500.

NOTE: (2) If a player is fouled and is subsequently ejected from the game before shooting the awarded free throw(s), he must immediately leave the court and another of the four players on the floor will be designated by the opposing coach to shoot such free throw(s).

NOTE: (3) When a foul is committed by an opponent of a player who as part of a continuous motion which started before the foul occurred, succeeds in making a goal, the goal shall count even if the ball leaves the player's hands after the whistle blows. The player must, in the opinion of the officials be throwing for a goal or starting an effort at the time the foul occurs. The goal does not count if the time expires before the ball leaves the player's hand.

NOTE: (4) During the last two minutes of the game and any overtime period, all deliberate defensive fouls away from the play, except loose ball fouls will be treated as follows:

The foul is charged with no fine involved as a personal and team foul but treated as a **technical**. This technical may be shot by anyone and the team retains possession of the ball.

2. Free Throw Penalty Situations

a. Each team shall be limited to four team fouls per quarter. Team fouls charged to a team in excess of four will be penalized by an additional free throw except as hereinafter provided.

(1) The first four team fouls committed by a team in each quarter—no shots will be taken— the opponents shall put the ball into play at the sideline nearest where the foul oc- curred. (Not closer to endline than foul line extended.) The first three team fouls com- mitted in each over-time period—the ball shall be put into play in the same manner as in the first four quarters. Shooting, backcourt, elbowing and fighting (punching) fouls will carry their own penalties and are included in the team totals.

(2) During each over-time period the limitation shall be three personal fouls per team with an additional free throw for each foul in excess of three.

(3) If a team has not committed its quota of four team fouls during the first ten minutes of

each quarter or its three team fouls in the first three minutes of any overtime period it shall be permitted to incur one team foul during the last two minutes of each regular quarter and the last two minutes of any overtime period without penalty.

(4) If the excess foul calls for two free throws (flagrant, backcourt, unsuccessful field goal attempt, swinging of elbows) the penalty free throw shall be permitted if either of the two is unsuccessful.

(5) If the foul committed by a player calls for a single free throw after a successful field goal, one additional free throw is allowed if the shot is missed.

NOTE: (1) The highest number of points that may be scored by the same team in one play is three. Technical fouls or punching fouls are not considered a part of a one play situation.

NOTE: (2) Penalty free throws must be attempted by the player who attempted the original free throws.

Section IV — Double Fouls

a. On all double fouls, personal or technical, no free throws are attempted. Where double fouls are personal fouls a personal foul is charged to each player but not to team totals.

NOTE: (1) If the double foul is "on" the ball, play resumes with a jump ball between the involved players at the nearest jump ball circle.

NOTE: (2) If the double foul is "off" the ball, the team that had possession of the ball at the time of the call retains possession. Play is resumed at a point out of bounds nearest where the play was interrupted and the 24-second clock is reset to 24 seconds.

NOTE: (3) If the ball is in the air when a double foul occurs and the field goal is unsuccessful, there will be a jump ball at the nearest free throw circle between the two players involved. If the goal is successful, the team that has been scored upon will put the ball into play at the end line, as after any score.

Section V — Offensive Fouls

All personal fouls by players of the offensive team shall be penalized as follows: Personal foul charged against the offensive player, ball awarded to the opponent out of bounds at a point nearest to where foul occurred. Official must handle ball. No charge is made to team total.

Section VI — Loose Ball Fouls

A personal foul committed while the ball is in the air for a shot or during rebounding and where there is no ball possession will be treated in the following manner: The offending team will be charged with a team foul, the offending player with a personal foul, no shot will be taken and the team fouled will retain possession. All other loose balls will be treated in a similar manner. If such foul occurs during a penalty situation all shots that apply on the personal will be attempted.

NOTE: When a "loose ball" foul is called against the defensive team that is then followed by a successful field goal (or successful foul try), the foul shot will be attempted, allowing for the 3 point play. This applies regardless which offensive player is fouled. If a foul is called against the offensive team during this type of situation, the original rule applies (no shot and possession).

Section VII — Fighting Fouls

A foul called against a player for punching or fighting is to be charged as a team foul and a personal foul where only one player is involved. However, the penalty situation does not apply and whether the foul try is made or missed, the ball shall be given to the team shooting the attempt at mid-court. If **two players** are involved the fouls are technical and no shots will be attempted as in

Rules

any other double foul situation. It is the official's decision whether or not the offending player or players shall be ejected. Whether or not said player or players are ejected, a fine not exceeding $10,000 and/or suspension may be imposed upon such player(s) by the Commissioner at his sole discretion.

NOTE: (1) This rule applies whether the play is in progress or ball is dead.

NOTE: (2) In the case where one punching foul is followed by another, all aspects of the rule are applied in both cases, and the team last offended is awarded possession.

---

1. Federation — Zone defenses are legal.
   NCAA — Zone defenses are legal.
   NBA — Zone defenses are illegal.
2. Federation — No monetary fines for penalties.
   NCAA — No monetary fines for penalties.
   NBA — Fines are assessed in conjunction with other penalties.
3. Federation — Two shots for field goal thrower, intentional foul, and flagrant foul.
   NCAA — Two shots for field goal thrower, intentional foul, and flagrant foul.
   NBA — Two shots for field goal thrower, intentional foul, flagrant foul, and backcourt foul.
4. Federation — Bonus rule goes into effect on the fifth team foul in each half.
   NCAA — Bonus rule goes into effect on the seventh team foul in each half.
   NBA — Bonus rule goes into effect on the fifth team foul in each quarter.
5. Federation — Bonus rule only applies to common fouls.
   NCAA — Bonus rule only applies to common fouls.
   NBA — Bonus rule applies to common and shooting fouls.

CHAPTER V

Illustrated Basketball Rules

The following illustrations of the rules are presented to supplement the rules and to clarify any question the official might have. It is hoped that they will provide a method to ease the transition from the printed word of the rule book to the visual experience of the game.

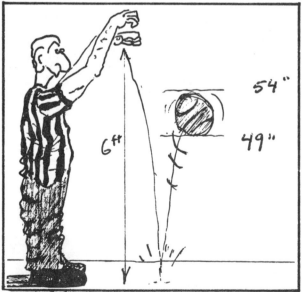

Court Ruling: The ball must be inflated so that when it is dropped to the court surface from six feet, it will rebound not less than 49 inches nor more than 54 inches measured from the top of the ball.

The referees have the power to make decisions on any point not specifically covered in the rules. Rule 2 Section 3.

Question: A violation and a foul occur at the same time. Both are observed by the same official, or the violation by one and the foul by the other. What is the proper procedure? *Answer:* The foul takes precedence. Rule 2 Section 4.

Blocking is personal contact which impedes the progress of an opponent. Rule 4 Section 2.

NCAA—NFHS Ruling: Any time a player in control of the ball is closely guarded for five seconds in the mid-court area, a held ball occurs.

A double tap during a dribble is illegal. It becomes a violation at the point of the second tap. Rule 4 Section 3.

A personal foul is a foul which involves contact with an opponent. Rule 4 Section 4a.

It is a violation to pick up your pivot foot prior to starting your dribble. Rule 4 Secion 9c-2.

An offensive foul is a foul committed by a player while he or a teammate is in control of the ball. Rule 4 Section 4d.

It is legal for a player to lift his pivot foot when shooting the ball. Rule 4 Section 9c-1.

Court Ruling:
A time-out is charged for searching for lost contact lens. No official's time-out should be permitted to allow any player to adjust his clothing or equipment (e.g. shoes, glasses, etc.) Rule 5 Section 4q.

Court Ruling: Question—Is it traveling if a player falls to the floor while holding the ball? Answer—No. Unless he makes progress by sliding. Rule 5 Section 9c.

If time runs out before the ball is in flight, a goal which is subsequently made doesn't count. Rule 5 Section 3a-1.

NCAA—NFHS Ruling: If the score is tied or the defense is behind, it is the defense responsibility to provide action. After Number 4 keeps the ball in the mid-court area for ten seconds, the official should call "Play ball" and point toward the direction the defense should advance.

The ball becomes dead when it lodges between the basket and the backboard. Rule 6 Section 6a(1). In the case of a ball which is lodged, a jump ball shall be held at the circle closest to the backboard where the ball is lodged. Rule 6 Section 4a(5).

It is a violation for an individual to hit a jump ball before it reaches its highest point. Rule 6 Section 5c.

During a jump ball, a jumper may top the ball twice. Rule 6 Section 5f.

On a jump ball, the eight now-jumpers may not violate the plane of the circle prior to the ball being legally tapped. Rule 6 Section 5g.

The ball becomes dead when a foul occurs. Rule 6 Section 6a-4.

A player is out of bounds when he touches the floor or any object on or outside a boundary. Rule 8 Section 1a

Court Ruling:
Number 5's throw in hits opponent and rebounds back and strikes Number 5 who is still out-of-bounds. Violation by Number 5 and ball is awarded to opponents for a throw-in.

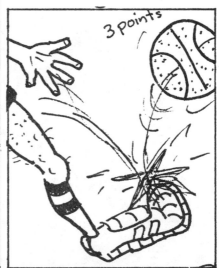

After a goal, a player is permitted to run along the end line to make a throw-in. Rule 8 Section 3c.

Kicking the ball is a violation when it is a positive (on purpose) act; accidentally striking the ball with the foot or leg is not a violation. Rule 10 Section 1d.

A player shall not touch the ball or basket when the ball is on or within *either* basket. Rule 11 Section 1a.

A player shall not make contact with the ball on its downward flight. Rule 11 Section 1c.

A player may not trap the ball against the face of the backboard. Rule 11 Section 1f.

Officials may penalize, without prior warning, any act of unsportsmanlike conduct by anyone seated on the bench which in the opinion of the officials, is detrimental to the game. Rule 12 Section 6a.

It is a personal foul if a player pushes his opponent to receive a pass. Rule 12B Section 1a.

The dribbler may not use his arm to ward off his opponent. Rule 12B Section 1a.

A dribbler shall not charge into or contact an opponent in his path or dribble between an opponent and a boundary unless the space is such to provide a reasonable chance for him to go through without contact. Rule 12B Section 2.

All personal fouls by players of the offensive team shall be penalized as follows: Personal foul charged against the offensive player, ball awarded to the opponent out of bounds at a point nearest to where foul occurred. Official must handle the ball. Rule 12B Section 5.

Glossary

BACKBOARD — the flat, rigid surface normally rectangular or fan-shaped, to which the basket is attached.

BACKCOURT — the half of the playing court opposite the offensive basket.

BASKET — the 18" ring, all the bracing attachments, and the attached net through which players attempt to throw the ball.

BLOCKING — contact that impedes the progress or direction of an opponent.

BONUS FREE THROW — second free throw awarded after a team accumulates a specific number of personal fouls, assuming the first free throw is unsuccessful.

CAPTAIN — the team representative designated to confer with the officials about rule interpretations or informational items.

CENTER CIRCLE — a circle with an inside radius of 2' located at the exact center of the playing court.

CHANGE OF STATUS — the time at which the ball either changes from being a live ball to a dead ball or vice versa.

DEAD BALL — a temporarily out-of-play ball.

DISQUALIFIED PLAYER — a player banned for further participation in the game.

DIVISION LINE — a 2" wide line separating the court into two equal parts extending through the center circle from sideline to sideline.

DRIBBLE — the act of bouncing, throwing, batting, or tossing the ball to the floor while retaining control once or several times.

DUNKING — carrying the ball into the area above the ring and forcing it down through the ring with one or both hands.

END LINE — the line connecting the sidelines forming a rectangular playing area that makes the court.

EXTRA PERIOD — an extension of the second half used to break a tie score.

FORFEIT — the ability of the referee to declare one team the winning team.

FORE-COURT — area of the court between the mid-court area marker and the end line at the offensive end of the court.

FOUL — an infraction of the rules

> **common foul** — a foul by a player that is neither flagrant, intentional, part of a double or multiple foul, nor inflicted against a player in the act of trying for a goal.
>
> **double foul** — two players fouling each other at the same time.
>
> **false double foul** — a foul against both teams, the second occuring before the clock is started after the first, but the fouls are separated by a period of time.
>
> **flagrant foul** — an unsportsmanlike act of either a violent nature or one which displays abusive conduct.
>
> **intentional foul** — a foul which is deliberate.
>
> **multiple foul** — two or more fouls committed by players of the same team against one opposing player.
>
> **personal foul** — a foul involving contact with an opponent during a live ball.
>
> **player control foul** — a foul by an offensive player while either he or his team is in control of the ball.
>
> **technical foul** — a foul by a player or non-player, including fans, coaches, and team attendents, that does not involve contact, but is viewed to be unsportsmanlike.

FREE THROW — an unmolested shot awarded to a player in an attempt to score one point as a result of a foul.

FREE THROW LANE — the area 12' wide and 19' long extending into the court from each endline centered beneath each basket.

FREE THROW LINE — a line which is 15' from the basket and marks the end of the free throw lane.

Glossary

FRONT COURT—the half of the court from the division line to the end line where the team is on offense.

FUMBLE—unintentional loss of control of the ball.

GOAL—the scoring of two points by causing the ball to go through the basket.

HELD BALL—a held ball occurs when the two opponents firmly grasp the ball simultaneously.

HOLDING—contact between opponents that illegally interferes with freedom of movement.

INTERMISSION—the period of time between either the quarters or halves.

JUMP BALL—same as held ball.

LACK OF SUFFICIENT ACTION—the failure of the responsible team to force the action.

LIVE BALL—the ball is alive when it leaves the official's hand on a jump ball, touches a player in bounds following a throw-in, or when handed to a free thrower.

LOCATION OF PLAYER—where the player is touching the floor or if he is in the air, the last place he touched the floor.

MID COURT—the area from the mid court marker to the division line in the offensive end of the court.

MULTIPLE THROW—two or more consecutive free throws attempted by the same team.

NET—a white cord 12-mesh net, 15" to 18" in length, suspended from beneath the ring.

OFFICIAL—a referee, one or two umpires, a scorer, and a timer, who as a team are responsible for the conduct of the game.

OUT-OF-BOUNDS—when a player or the ball touches the floor or any object outside the boundary lines of the court.

PENALTY—the resulting action from either a violation or foul.

PERIOD—the time divisions for any game, either quarters or halves.

PIVOT—the action used to evade an opponent by moving in either direction while keeping the same foot stationary.

PLAYER CONTROL—a player is in control when he or his teammates are holding or dribbling the ball.

REFEREE—the official who holds ultimate responsibility for the game.

RESTRAINING CIRCLE—a circle drawn concentrically around the center circle with an outside radius of 6'.

RESTRAINING LINE—a broken line used as a temporary boundary line on courts with restricted out-of-bounds area.

RULE—one of the laws governing the action of the game.

SCORER—the off-floor official designated to keep the records of the game in the official scorebook.

SCREEN—a maneuver used by a teammate to impede the direction of a guarding opponent.

SIDELINE—the lines used to connect the endlines forming a rectangular court.

TEAM CONTROL—a team is in control when a player of the team is in control or the ball is being passed between teammates.

THROW IN—method of putting the ball in play.

TIMER—the off-court official designated to keep the time on the official timepiece.

TRAVELING—carrying the ball more than one step without dribbling, passing, or shooting.

TRY—an attempt to cause the ball to go through the ring from above.

UMPIRE—the official(s) who works as the equal of the referee in officiating the game.

VIOLATION—a minor infraction of the rules resulting in loss of possession of the ball.